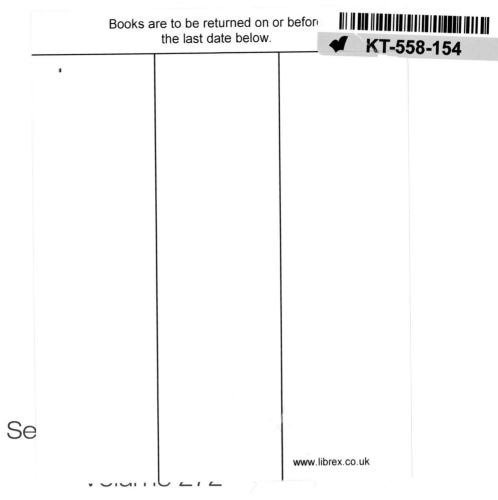

Se

www.librex.co.uk

Volume 272

Independence

First published by Independence Educational Publishers

The Studio, High Green

Great Shelford

Cambridge CB22 5EG

England

© Independence 2015

Copyright

Photocopy licence

British Library Cataloguing in Publication Data

Gambling. -- (Issues ; 272)

1. Gambling--Great Britain. 2. Compulsive gamblers--Great

Britain.

I. Series II. Acred, Cara editor.

363.4'2'0941-dc23

ISBN-13: 9781861687005

Printed in Great Britain

Zenith Print Group

Contents

Introduction

Gambling is Volume 272 in the *ISSUES* series. The aim of the series is to offer current, diverse information about important issues in our world, from a UK perspective.

ABOUT GAMBLING

The number of betting shops in the UK increased by 1.3% in 2013, and with people gambling in amounts up to £3 million there is increasing concern about problem gambling and the risks associated with it. This book explores the way that changing communication technologies have influenced the gambling industry and what 'problem gambling' really means to those affected by it. It also examines gambling laws and the help available for those with addictions.

OUR SOURCES

Titles in the *ISSUES* series are designed to function as educational resource books, providing a balanced overview of a specific subject.

The information in our books is comprised of facts, articles and opinions from many different sources, including:

⇨ Newspaper reports and opinion pieces

⇨ Website factsheets

⇨ Magazine and journal articles

⇨ Statistics and surveys

⇨ Government reports

⇨ Literature from special interest groups.

A NOTE ON CRITICAL EVALUATION

Because the information reprinted here is from a number of different sources, readers should bear in mind the origin of the text and whether the source is likely to have a particular bias when presenting information (or when conducting their research). It is hoped that, as you read about the many aspects of the issues explored in this book, you will critically evaluate the information presented.

It is important that you decide whether you are being presented with facts or opinions. Does the writer give a biased or unbiased report? If an opinion is being expressed, do you agree with the writer? Is there potential bias to the 'facts' or statistics behind an article?

ASSIGNMENTS

In the back of this book, you will find a selection of assignments designed to help you engage with the articles you have been reading and to explore your own opinions. Some tasks will take longer than others and there is a mixture of design, writing and research-based activities that you can complete alone or in a group.

FURTHER RESEARCH

At the end of each article we have listed its source and a website that you can visit if you would like to conduct your own research. Please remember to critically evaluate any sources that you consult and consider whether the information you are viewing is accurate and unbiased.

Useful weblinks

www.aquarius.org.uk

www.bigdeal.org.uk

www.bigissue.com

www.cam.ac.uk (University of Cambridge)

www.casinolifemagazine.com

www.cnwl.nhs.uk

www.gambleaware.co.uk

www.gamblingwatchuk.org

www.gamcare.org.uk

www.gordonmoody.org.uk

www.helpguide.org

www.mentalhealthfoundation.org.uk

www.nhs.uk

www.ntu.ac.uk (Nottingham Trent University)

www.rga.eu.com (Responsible Gambling Association)

www.sbcnews.co.uk

www.tes.co.uk (Times Educational Supplement)

Gambling

Why do we gamble?

People gamble for a whole range of reasons including:

⇨ the buzz, the excitement, and the high adrenaline release

⇨ the competitive element – trying to beat other players, the bookie or the dealer

⇨ the thrill of risk taking, of placing large bets

⇨ to solve financial problems

⇨ a way of escaping from stress or worries.

Sensible gambling

Some people say that there is no such thing as safe gambling. Others argue that gambling is like drinking alcohol – it's safe to do as long as you follow some sensible rules:

⇨ Keep away from high-risk forms of gambling where you can lose large sums of money very quickly.

⇨ Limit the amount of time you gamble. This will give you time to do other, more important things with your life.

⇨ Limit the amount you spend to the amount you can afford to lose. When you have spent this much, walk away.

⇨ Quit while you are ahead. If you continue, you are likely to lose because the odds are always stacked against you. That's how bookies and the casinos make their money.

When gambling becomes a problem

For most of us, gambling is a harmless activity. But, for some people, gambling is a way of life, an addiction that can wreck their lives.

You may be a compulsive gambler if:

⇨ you spend more money on gambling than you can afford. If you continue to gamble, you could get into serious debt. You could also lose your home and your possessions

⇨ you spend so much time gambling that you neglect other important areas of your life, like your family or your work. You could lose your job or end up divorced or separated from your partner and children

⇨ your feelings and behaviour change. For example, you may become depressed when you lose or over-excited when you win. In serious cases, you may feel that you are only really alive when you gamble

⇨ it leads you to inappropriate or even criminal behaviour. For example, you may lie to family and friends about your gambling activities or you may steal to fund your gambling habit.

Questions to ask yourself

If you think you may have a gambling problem but are not sure, ask yourself:

⇨ Is gambling making me unhappy at work or at home?

⇨ Is gambling making it hard to sleep at night or concentrate during the day?

⇨ Am I lying to other people and myself about how much I gamble?

⇨ Am I gambling to get away from problems or worries?

⇨ Am I gambling to get money – so that I can pay off debts or solve financial problems?

⇨ Am I borrowing money or selling possessions so that I can gamble?

⇨ If I have just won or just lost, do I feel I need to gamble just a little bit more?

If you answered yes to any of these questions, then you may have a gambling problem.

What causes compulsive gambling?

All compulsive behaviours have social, psychological and biological origins. Gambling brings us into contact with others, even if we are using Internet gaming rooms. This can provide a sense of community, however damaging the associated behaviours. Social meaning and acceptance by others are important to us all and for the compulsive gambler these can be found in virtual gaming rooms, real casinos, bookmakers and so on.

Gambling also changes how we feel psychologically as well as socially. It allows us to escape our normal lives and the everyday struggles we experience. During a period of gambling our mind is occupied by the odds, the bet, the race, the actions of other gamers, the run of the cards and so on. It can be all-consuming and therefore provides an engaging, exciting escape from ordinary life.

At the biological level, compulsive behaviours can have a direct effect on the brain's dopamine reward system. This system regulates our responses to natural rewards like food, sex and social interaction. Repeated compulsive behaviours can act on this system with a power and persistence that changes its cells chemically and structurally. This in turn can have an overwhelming effect on our well-being. People may no longer respond normally to rewards such as food, sex and social interaction, and instead depend on gambling for their sense of reward.

Compulsive gambling can therefore develop through the social meaning and psychological relief that it offers. This is further compounded by the chemical changes in our brain that accompany these experiences. It is in fact artificial to separate these factors since they all occur simultaneously for the compulsive gambler. Social meaning, psychological relief and a fired dopamine reward system can be a difficult combination of experiences for the most hardy of individuals to resist.

Helping yourself

If you feel that you have lost control of your gambling, there are some things you can do to help yourself.

⇨ Admitting you have a problem is the first and most important step.

⇨ Find someone you can trust to talk to about your problem. It could be a friend, a relative or a specialist advisor.

⇨ Avoid locations and situations where you may be tempted to gamble.

⇨ Take control of how you spend your money, so that you don't waste it on gambling.

⇨ If you can't do this by yourself, you may need to ask someone else to help you do this.

⇨ Take one day at a time. Don't expect everything to improve straight away.

Living with someone who gambles

Living with someone who gambles can be just as difficult as living with someone with any other kind of addiction. It can be very stressful and it can lead to the breakdown of your relationship.

If you are not sure whether you are living with someone who has a gambling problem, ask yourself:

⇨ Do they promise time and time again to stop gambling but carry on anyway?

⇨ Do they disappear for long periods of time without telling you where they were?

⇨ Do they spend large sums of money without being able to account for it?

⇨ Do you hide money to stop them spending it?

⇨ Do they lie to cover up or deny their gambling?

If you answered yes to most of these questions, then they may have a gambling problem.

How to help someone who gambles

It is important to remember you are not the only person in this situation and there are lots of people who can help.

⇨ Talk it through with the other person and, if necessary, get professional help.

⇨ Be firm and constructive. You need to make sure the other person actually faces the problem but also has some ideas of how to move things forward.

⇨ Do not condemn them or try to make them feel bad about themselves. Just telling them to 'snap out of it' may not help and could actually make it worse.

⇨ Be realistic. Compulsive gambling is an addiction, so it will take them time to overcome it. Some days will be better than others.

⇨ Do not trust them with money until they have overcome the addiction.

⇨ The above information is reprinted with kind permission from the Mental Health Foundation (2014). Please visit www.mentalhealth.org.uk for further information.

How gambling works

Whether playing a slot machine or buying a scratchcard, it helps to know your chances of winning. This article will help you understand what is meant by odds and probability, so you can make informed decisions about the money you are spending when gambling.

What's the chance you're going to win?

Probability is the likelihood of a specific outcome or event taking place. To work this out, you divide the number of specific outcomes with the number of possible outcomes.

For example, if you were rolling a dice and wanted the number three to come up, there is only one specific outcome; at the same time, there are six possible outcomes because the dice could land on one, two, three, four, five or six. So the probability of you rolling a three is one in six.

Randomness

Randomness means that each possible outcome has the same chance, or probability, of occurring.

For example:

⇨ When you roll a dice, the probability of rolling a two is the same as the probability of rolling a six, which is the same probability of rolling any of the other numbers. So you could say that the chance of rolling a specific number is one in six.

⇨ When you flip a coin, the probability of it landing on heads is the same as the probability of it landing on tails, so you could say that it has a 50% chance or it's 50/50.

The reason each outcome is as likely as all of the others is that it all depends on chance. If a flipped coin landed on heads several times in a row, it's easy to think that it has to come up tails on the next flip. However, the coin doesn't 'remember' what it has landed on before in the same way that it doesn't 'decide' what to land on next. No matter what has happened already, the probability of it landing on heads or tales is always 50/50. Unless you can see the future, the result of a rolled dice or flipped coin is unknown and unpredictable, so we can say that the outcome is random.

Remember: despite what you might think, you can't work out or control an outcome that's based on chance and randomness – people who try to do this often lose a lot of money. They might win now and then, but this is also down to chance. Thinking that you can beat the system can cause big problems.

Odds and house edge

In gambling, the 'odds' are the chances a person has of winning a bet, but these always work against that person.

The 'house' refers to the people who offer the bet (the casino, bookmaker, slot machine owner, etc.) and they always have the 'edge'. This means that the designers of the machine or game make sure that it works in their favour and they will always make money overall.

In every betting game, the odds are against the player. Every person who hits the jackpot on a slot machine is actually winning money that previous players lost. Sadly, the longer you gamble, the more likely it is that you will lose money, because the odds are against you. Many problem gamblers have the false belief that they will be able to 'beat the system' but over time they'll lose money, probably an awful lot of it.

The odds of winning the National Lottery jackpot are about one in 14 million. Think of it like this: your friend Dave lives somewhere in London and you want to call him at home but don't have his number. If you try reaching him by dialling one of 12.5 million London phone numbers, your odds of getting his number right on the first try are better than the odds of winning the lottery jackpot.

Skill or chance?

Some forms of gambling are down to chance, and some may involve some skill. Here's a breakdown:

Chance

⇨ Lottery, Euromillions, etc.

⇨ Scratchcards

⇨ Bingo

⇨ Roulette

⇨ Slot machines.

Skill (at least partially)

⇨ Blackjack

⇨ Poker

⇨ Horse racing

⇨ Sports betting.

⇨ The above information is reprinted with kind permission from GamCare. GamCare is the leading provider of information, advice, support and free counselling for the prevention and treatment of problem gambling. GamCare staff are fully trained and give confidential guidance to anyone affected by a gambling problem. Freephone 0808 8020133 or visit www.gamcare.org.uk for further information.

Types of gambling

Slot machines

Slot machines can be found in most pubs, amusement arcades and other locations. The player inserts money and presses buttons to make the reels spin round. The combination of pictures that line up when they've stopped spinning means you've either lost or won, although sometimes the machine might have a bonus feature to keep the game going a little longer. Slot machines are also called fruit machines because the pictures on the reels are often lemons, cherries, pineapples and so on. The whole game is down to a random number generator, which means that you can never guess the outcome.

Lottery

There are many different types of lotteries but they all work around the same system. Whether it's the National Lottery, Thunderball, EuroMillions or even a raffle ticket you've bought at the local church, some of the people that take part will win money or prizes, whilst most won't win anything at all.

The National Lottery in the UK is drawn every Wednesday and Saturday. A player picks six numbers from one to 49 or asks for a lucky dip, which is when the ticket machine chooses the numbers randomly for you. The quantity of your chosen numbers that match the ones drawn during that particular game determines how much you've won, if anything at all: three matching numbers wins you £25, four and five wins you more, and all six wins you the jackpot. However, even though you only need to match six numbers to win big, the chance of being a jackpot winner is one in just under 14 million. To put this into perspective, you are 24 times more likely to be struck by lightning – but fingers crossed that'll never happen.

The EuroMillions is drawn every Tuesday and Friday and requires a player to pick five main numbers from one to 50 and two lucky star numbers from one to 11. You can win a lot more in this game, but the odds of winning the jackpot are one in over 116 million. As a comparison, you are one of 62 million people in the UK (far less than 116 million), which makes you realise just how small the chances of winning the jackpot are. True, someone has to win, but many more have to lose. It's for you to decide if you want to risk your money and in the end it's your call; that's why we want you to know how it all works.

Scratchcards

A scratchcard is a small piece of card with a thin covering that can be scratched away using a coin. Scratchcards are available at different prices, usually starting at £1, and the more expensive the card, the larger the prizes available or the higher the chance of the player winning one. Sometimes a symbol beneath the scratchable area has to match a particular type, and sometimes three of the same symbol or monetary amounts need to be uncovered in order to win. Either way, the player may have a higher chance of winning on a scratchcard than the lottery, but the prizes are smaller and there's still a larger chance that nothing will be won at all.

Poker

In poker, two or more players are given cards that have been shuffled at random. They then bet on the value of their cards, which is called their 'hand', and bets are placed in the 'pot' in the middle of the table. A player wins everyone's bets by having the highest amount using two cards in their hand and three on the table. Players try to force others to 'fold', meaning they've dropped out of the game and lost their bets. Poker does require some skill, but in the end only one player can win and chance plays a large part.

Blackjack

Blackjack is a relatively simple card game. A player is dealt cards one by one with the aim of their combined value (one, two, three, etc.) adding up to as close to 21 as possible without going over. If your cards add up to over 21 you automatically lose – this is called 'busting'. But if they add up to under 21 whilst being higher than that of the other player or dealer, you win. One of the risks of blackjack is that it's very easy to keep taking another card, or a 'hit', which will usually result in you busting and your opponent winning the game.

Roulette

Roulette is a game in which the croupier (casino host) spins a ball around a wheel which has 37 red or black numbered holes around its circumference. Players may choose to place bets on the ball landing on either a single number or a range of numbers, the colours red or black, or whether the number is odd or even. The odds at which each outcome pays out depends on the probability of that outcome happening.

Bingo

Bingo is a game in which players are given cards with random numbers printed on them. The bingo caller shouts out numbers one by one as they're removed from the ball machine, and the player marks off each number if it's on their card. The winner is the first person to mark off five numbers in a row or another required pattern.

Bingo is all down to chance – the numbers on your cards and the numbers drawn from the machine are

entirely random – but you also need to listen up because if you miss your number when it's called out, it's game over.

Sports betting and racing

There are various types of bets that you can place on sports, most of which can be made at betting shops, also known as bookmakers or bookies. The odds of an individual sportsperson, team, horse or dog are provided and you can bet your money on them, but even if they're expected to win it doesn't mean they definitely will.

If, for example, a horse is a strong runner, it might be given odds of 2/1, meaning that if you bet £1 and it wins, you'll get £2 back plus your original stake (so £3 overall). Meanwhile, if another horse is expected to lose and is given odds of 100/1, if you bet £1 and it wins, you'll get £100 back plus your original stake (so £101 overall). However, chance always plays a large part in all games and bets: the horse that people expect to win may slow down or even fall over, and the horse with poor odds may have more energy than usual and beat all of the others. Or maybe not: there are so many things that could happen, so just remember to gamble responsibly.

Online gambling

Most of the types of gambling described here can also be found online as well as in shops, arcades or casinos, and virtual forms of gambling share many of the same features as offline, or land-based, gambling.

⇨ The above information is reprinted with kind permission from GamCare. GamCare is the leading provider of information, advice, support and free counselling for the prevention and treatment of problem gambling. GamCare staff are fully trained and give confidential guidance to anyone affected by a gambling problem. Freephone 0808 8020133 or visit www.gamcare.org.uk for further information.

© GamCare 2014

Myths and facts

The more you gamble, the more likely it is that you'll have a big win

That's like saying you're more likely to win if you put £100 down instead of £1. It's all down to chance: the longer the amount of time spent gambling will usually mean paying more for that leisure time.

If you keep playing for long enough, you'll eventually win all your money back

Actually, the more you gamble, the more likely it is you'll lose more money. The odds are always stacked in favour of those offering the bet – the bookies, casinos and lottery companies know that some people will win, but more people have to lose so that the companies can stay in business.

Knowing a game well increases your chances of winning

Again, it's all down to chance. Games such as poker and sports betting can benefit from extra knowledge, but you still can't guess the outcome. You might think you're the best poker player around, but someone else may be better or have stronger cards. Your football team might have won the last two matches, but that doesn't mean they'll win a third. Remember to always play it safe.

When gambling, keeping track of previous results can help you figure out the coming results

There is no pattern when it comes to gambling. If there were a pattern, everyone would learn it and no one would ever lose. If no one lost there'd be no money left in the slot machines, and the bookies and casinos would become bankrupt and wouldn't be able to pay the winners. Believing these rumours will only cause you to lose lots of cash and stop gambling from being fun.

Young people don't have gambling problems

Anyone who gambles may be at risk of developing a gambling problem, including young people. Two per cent of young people in the UK (that's 60,000 young people) are likely to be struggling with a gambling problem this very moment. That could be someone you know.

⇨ The above information is reprinted with kind permission from GamCare. GamCare is the leading provider of information, advice, support and free counselling for the prevention and treatment of problem gambling. GamCare staff are fully trained and give confidential guidance to anyone affected by a gambling problem. Freephone 0808 8020133 or visit www.gamcare.org. uk for further information.

© GamCare 2014

UK's gambling habits: what's really happening?

As MPs debate the impact of fixed-odds betting machines, we look at the data to find out which forms of gambling are the most popular in which parts of the country – and what has changed.

By Mona Chalabi

Labour is to press the Coalition on their gambling policy on Wednesday during an opposition day debate. Ed Miliband has said Labour would give councils the power to ban high-stakes roulette machines from bookmakers' shops, and the party wants the Government to adopt similar plans.

The gambling industry has been accused of focusing these roulette machines (known as fixed-odds betting terminals, or FOBTs) in the UK's poorer areas, reaping enormous financial rewards in the process. We look at the evidence on those claims.

How much do companies earn from fixed-odds machines?

The Gambling Commission, using data provided by bookmakers, estimated there were 33,284 FOBTs in betting shops located across the UK in 2012. The declared gross profit from these machines was £1.42 billion last year, meaning the average weekly profit per machine was £825, up from £760 in 2011.

How much does the Government earn from fixed-odds machines?

Last month, HMRC also published statistics on how much the Government earns from betting taxes. The figures are considerable:

⇨ in 2012–13, the Government received £1.7 billion in betting and gaming duties, representing 0.4% of all HMRC revenue. For comparison, HMRC earned £26.6 billion from fuel duty and £41 billion from corporation tax during the same period.

⇨ £831 million comes from lottery duties and £75 million from bingo but the total government revenue from machine games is currently nil. A tax on these machines was not introduced until 1 February 2013, so no revenues have yet been recorded from this mode of gaming.

Where is gambling most popular?

An analysis for *The Guardian* last year found that northern, urban cities and London boroughs with high levels of unemployment bet four times more on gambling machines than richer rural areas in southern England where jobless numbers are low.

There were 9,128 operating betting shops in 2012 with an average of 3.65 fixed-odds machines each.

Which methods of gambling are the most popular?

Four times a year, the Gambling Commission takes a survey of more than 4,000 adults whose demographics are representative of the UK as a whole. In the latest survey, bingo and lottery draws are the most popular form of gambling – but the trends look very different based on frequency.

Virtual gaming machines in a bookmakers are the third most popular form of gambling for those who do so more than twice a week.

Who gambles?

The Gambling Commission regularly conducts surveys to find out about British gambling habits. They ask respondents if they have participated in at least one form of gambling in the previous four weeks. The latest results show that 55% of the UK gambles, down from 57% in 2012.

But people aged 18 to 24 buck the downward trend; they are now almost 5% more likely to gamble than they were a year ago.

8 January 2014

⇨ The above information is reprinted with kind permission from *The Guardian*. Please visit www.theguardian.com for further information.

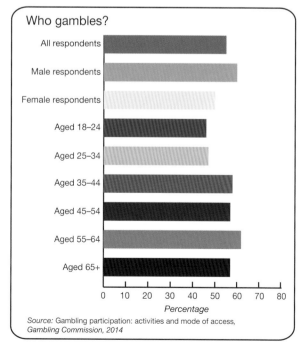

Who gambles?

- All respondents
- Male respondents
- Female respondents
- Aged 18–24
- Aged 25–34
- Aged 35–44
- Aged 45–54
- Aged 55–64
- Aged 65+

0 10 20 30 40 50 60 70 80

Percentage

Source: Gambling participation: activities and mode of access, Gambling Commission, 2014

'Gambling professor explains British casino culture'

Dr Mark Griffiths on UK Gambling: 'We aren't unique. But we're relaxed and tolerant.'

Sam Miranda sat down with Professor of Gambling Studies at Nottingham Trent University and co-founder of GamCare Dr Mark Griffiths to discuss the British gambling industry. Topics ranged from casino culture to operator responsibilities. *Casino Life*'s Sam Miranda has the scoop...

By Dr Mark Griffiths' own admission, his path into gambling-related academia was 'boring'. He was given three options for his PhD – gynaecological psychology, face processing and gambling.

The industry is eternally grateful he chose the latter – in a 27-year career, Dr Griffiths has emerged as Britain's chief gambling authority, with his personal blog recently surpassing one million unique visitors. A chartered psychologist by vocation, his impressive oeuvre spans slot and video game addiction, adolescent gaming and socially responsible gambling. Dr Griffiths juggles media commitments – he pens regular columns in *The Sun* and *The Independent* and recalls a 'pleasant' interview with the feisty Jeremy Paxman – with a number of advisory and consultancy roles.

Does Dr Griffiths' focus on addiction mean he is anti-gambling? No. Any media statements to the contrary have been taken out of context. Dr Griffiths champions a well-regulated, socially responsible gambling industry, where an appreciation for personal liberties and support for an economically empowering sector are coupled with protection for vulnerable players.

Dr Griffiths, thanks for joining us. To start us off, can you summarise the research you do?

I've spent the last 27 years studying gambling, mainly problem gambling.

Not that I'm anti-gambling in the slightest. People often perceive me as being public enemy number one because I research problem gambling. Yet my friends who research problem drinking – no one accuses them of being anti-drinking.

There is a culture in this country that if you in anyway attack the industry for the products that they put out and highlight the plight of problem gamblers, they take it personally. We should be working together. Problem gamblers don't support a long-term, sustainable business model because they have a short shelf life. We have a situation where ten per cent of customers generate 90 per cent of profits. I want to replicate Camelot's model for the lottery – where the vast majority of the population spends small amounts of money and it still generates huge profits – across the casino and bingo industries.

What would you say is unique about British gambling culture?

Having travelled around the world, I wouldn't say we're unique. But we're relaxed and tolerant.

The most profound change in British gambling culture came with the introduction of the National Lottery in 1994. Suddenly two thirds of the public were gambling, but there was a mismatch between people viewing playing the lottery as a form of gambling. You would ask people, 'Do you gamble?' and they'd say 'No'. But then you would ask them, 'Do you play the lottery?' and they would say 'Yes'.

What followed was a drip drip effect. Football pools and bingo halls were saying, 'You've taken some of our custom away and you're not letting us advertise on television. We want an equal playing field.' This prompted a government

policy of liberalisation and de-regulation. But then casino and gambling operators asked, 'Why are scratch cards being advertised in the middle of *Coronation Street*? You the Home Office have just defined hard forms of gambling as ones which have high or rapid staking. You are allowing them to be advertised, so why can't we advertise our products?'

I would say in the past 15 years, gambling has become a socially acceptable activity. Now with remote opportunities, it's endemic. We were one of first countries that legalised Internet gambling. We've adopted a proactive, progressive stance. Yes, you still have your faith groups and people who have been adversely affected lobbying against it, but we're a gambling nation.

'We're a gambling nation.' Does that translate into high levels of problem gambling and addiction? The press would certainly make us believe so...

The press equates problem or pathological gambling with addiction. The British Gambling Prevalence Survey (BGPS) that we do every few years reveals that 0.9 per cent of Britain's have a gambling problem. The press have interpreted this as one per cent of people are addicted. All addicts are problem gamblers but not all problem gamblers are addicts. Problem gambling could just mean you spend too much of your disposable income on gambling, but this might not be indicative of addiction. The press use and interchange words to suit their story and lose all understanding of context. The number of people who are genuinely addicted is very small compared to, say, alcohol.

So is the British media anti-gambling?

It isn't anti-gambling per se, but they are running a business. If you're pointing out bad things like gambling addiction, people will read it. As human beings, we love reading about the suffering of others. It's called social comparison theory – when you read about the misery of others, it makes you feel better.

You've said gambling is endemic in British society. What have you discovered about different gambling demographics? Are people of a certain gender inclined to gamble on certain games?

Men gravitate towards skill games. It's interesting, because in Britain men are more likely to play slot games than women, whereas in other countries it's the same. We're the only country in the world which doesn't use a random number generator. This means that there's a level of skill involved – people can watch the machine fill up with other people's money, then come in and get the pay-out.

'In Britain men are more likely to play slot games than women, whereas in other countries it's the same'

We tracked down the machine patent and found out that they use adaptive logic and a compensator. In this country, single site machines are located in chip shops, pubs and cafes, and they're needed to keep the business afloat. RNG's work on a yearly cycle, and these places can't wait that long to recoup profits. So instead of probability cycles based on millions of spins, they are based on hundreds of thousands. This means you can watch a machine fill up with £300 of other peoples' money, and intervene at the right time. Although chance determined, there's an element of skill. Young males see it as a skill-based video game.

Let's move on to British casino culture. How would you describe the British casino as a social space?

The Gambling Act was a step in the right direction for diversifying the appeal of casinos. I can go in and have a cheap cordon bleu meal: ten pounds for good food. I can enjoy slightly subsidised alcohol and spend a couple of hours at the roulette table. That's four or five hours of entertainment with friends, and I've spent about £40. That's cheaper than watching Nottingham Forest lose, and cheaper than watching Noel Gallagher at the arena. It's great value. But the key is, I'm buying entertainment – I'm not going in with the goal of winning money.

Compared to international resorts like Las Vegas, Atlantic City and Macau, our casinos are small and parochial. You could fit 20 or 30 of them into a Las Vegas resort. UK casinos have a hard-core clientele – less than five per cent of the British public have visited a casino in the past year.

Why haven't we seen British casinos branch out into Vegas-style leisure and entertainment complexes?

We could have had super casinos. I was part of a committee that awarded a super casino to Manchester, based on the location and operators that offered the best infrastructure in terms of player protection, harm minimisation and social responsibility. But then you had Gordon Brown come in as Prime Minister, and as a Presbyterian he made the top-down decision to veto super casinos, arguing that there were other ways to regenerate local economies.

I think at some point, the Government is going to realise the need for super casinos. A cost-benefit analysis favoured a super casino in Manchester. I did some research for Canadian gaming organisations where we talked about a centralised gaming model, which is essentially destination resort gambling. In a way, having a mecca is the most socially responsible way of controlling gambling. People need to make a pre-commitment to go there and gamble. In this country, we have too many ambient gambling experiences. You go into a chip shop, and there's a slot machine, which means you gamble on impulse. Casinos and bingo halls are dedicated spaces.

Casinos are often described as an exercise in psychology. Can you provide some examples?

Any design of any commercial environment uses psychology. When it comes to design, there are lots of things. Floor plan is key – in Las Vegas, it took me half an hour to get to the auditorium to see a show, by which time I'd passed thousands of slot machines. The sound of winning maximises availability bias, and music with high beats per minute makes people spend more money. In the future, slot machines will look to harvest player data and preferences in order to offer personalise gaming experiences.

We conducted a study at Nottingham Trent University which showed gamblers spend more money under red light than white light. These environmental influences are good at getting you to gamble in the first place, but they have a negligible impact on problem gambling. It's the structural characteristics of the games that determine that.

You talk a lot about socially responsible gambling. What kinds of measures exist to ensure this? How are operators embracing responsible gambling?

I first coined the term in the mid-1990s. We're now at a point where you can't receive an operating licence in the UK unless you're displaying measures for protection and harm minimisation. We've come a long way. There are things to help players make informed decisions, and what I call the 'seatbelt approach' allows players to set limits or temporarily exclude themselves. We want players to pre-commit to how much they want to gamble in terms of time and money.

'I think at some point, the Government is going to realise the need for super casinos. A cost-benefit analysis favoured a super casino in Manchester'

Online behavioural tracking is now widely available, and in the physical space, Norway and Sweden are leading the way with player cards which log gambling activity. I've developed a product called GamGuard – adopted by 30 companies – that assesses the riskiness of a game according to the structural characteristics designed in to it. Companies have a traffic light system for whether their product is likely to be problematic to a susceptible individual. They can make a decision about whether to change its characteristics, and adjust the availability and marketing of the product accordingly.

We've seen a radical shift in the past ten years, with every major company agreeing to a code of conduct. Protective measures and protocols will become second nature.

30 January 2014

⇨ The above information was originally published by Ace Publishing Ltd. Please visit www.casinolifemagazine.com for further information.

Frequency of gambling in the past four weeks by activity type

Type of gambling activity and mode			Frequency of participation				
			2+ days a week	Once a week	Once a month, less than once a week	Less than once a month	Bases (weighted)
National Lottery draws	In person	%	18	50	24	8	1321
	Online	%	16	46	33	5	388
Another lottery	In person	%	4	24	36	35	486
	Online	%	4	24	61	11	93
Bingo	In person	%	10	41	31	18	76
	Online	%	[12]	[23]	[55]	[9]	21
Football pools	In person	%	17	60	13	10	89
	Online	%	20	45	26	10	53
Virtual dog or horse racing	In person	%	[11]	[21]	[-]	[68]	11
	Online	%	[-]	[100]	[-]	[-]	1
Spread betting	In person	%	[-]	[100]	[-]	[-]	1
	Online	%	[14]	[17]	[54]	[15]	8
Casino games	In person	%	7	14	24	[56	33
	Online	%	[38]	[12]	[23]	[28]	25
Any other activity	In person	%	[12]	[29]	[17]	[42]	26
	Online	%	[33]	[37]	[30]	[-]	2
Scratchcards		%	19	26	41	14	385
Fruit or slot machines		%	18	26	31	30	94
Virtual gaming machines in a bookmakers		%	21	36	20	24	64
Online slot machine style games/instant wins		%	[11]	[25]	[52]	[13]	26
Poker at a pub/club		%	[3]	[44]	[25]	[28]	15
Private betting		%	6	10	23	61	157

Source: Gambling participation: activities and mode of access, year to June 2014, *Gambling Comission, July 2014*

Gambling on smartphones

A blog post by C. S. Thurlbourn.

In 2012/13 GamCare answered 16,168 calls from problem gamblers and people affected by gambling, an increase of 2.8% from the previous year. The number of people gambling online also increased, from 23% in 2011/12 to 26% in 2012/13.

Online gambling is currently the second most popular method across all age groups and experts believe that a rise in mobile technology, such as 3G and 4G, will only fuel its accessibility – especially among the young.

According to H2 Gambling Capital, the global GGY (gross gaming yield) for remote gambling in 2011 was £20.1 billion, a 10% increase on the previous year. The Responsible Gambling Association says that remote gambling is the 'newest and fastest growing part of the world gambling industry' and that 'newer, cheaper and modern communication technologies will mean continued growth of online leisure services for which online gambling is one.' Ironically, however, the development of communication technologies has also helped to direct young people towards GamCare's youth-focused BigDeal website.

GamCare launched the BigDeal website (www.bigdeal. org.uk) in November 2012. It is specifically aimed at young people aged between 12 and 18 years old and is designed to offer advice and information about the risks of gambling. According to GamCare's statistical release, 20% of the site's visitors per month are via mobile devices, and Facebook is credited with helping them to engage with young people and direct them to the site.

So, it seems that the rise in smartphone technology presents us with a double-edged sword. While it makes gambling more readily available, it also promotes access to charities and organisations that provide help for problem gamblers.

Links

- Responsible Gambling Association: www.rga. eu.com

- GamCare: www.gamcare.org.uk

- BigDeal: www.bigdeal.org.uk

1 November 2014

⇨ The above information is reprinted with kind permission from C. S. Thurlbourn.

© C. S. Thurlbourn 2014

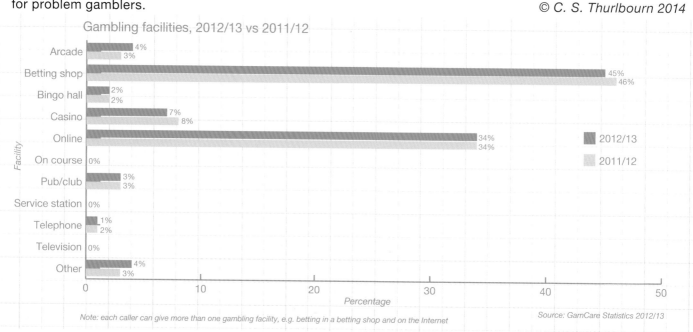

Gambling facilities, 2012/13 vs 2011/12

Facility	2012/13	2011/12
Arcade	4%	3%
Betting shop	45%	46%
Bingo hall	2%	2%
Casino	7%	8%
Online	34%	34%
On course	0%	
Pub/club	3%	3%
Service station	0%	
Telephone	1%	2%
Television	0%	
Other	4%	3%

Percentage

Note: each caller can give more than one gambling facility, e.g. betting in a betting shop and on the Internet

Source: GamCare Statistics 2012/13

Behaviour – online games can 'hook' children into gambling

Academic urges teachers to educate students about perils of play.

The rapid increase in the number of young people playing online computer games, often via social media sites, could lead to a surge in childhood gambling problems, a leading academic has warned.

Popular games are introducing teenagers to the excitement and rewards of gambling, even when they do not involve playing for money, according to Mark Griffiths, director of the International Gaming Research Unit at Nottingham Trent University in England.

Professor Griffiths, a world authority on gambling, believes that teachers have a vital role to play to ensure that children understand not only the potential rewards of gambling but also its risks. He wants to see gambling and gaming covered on the timetable during personal, social and health education (PSHE). Such lessons could explore the mechanics of gambling and the fact that there must always be more losers than winners, he said.

'I've always said that gambling and gaming is off the radar,' Professor Griffiths told TES. 'But teachers should start talking about these sorts of things. I don't want to come across as an omen of doom. There's nothing wrong with kids playing gambling-type games, but you have to accompany it with education.'

Many social media websites offer opportunities to play online poker with virtual money. Similarly, cash-gambling sites offer free-play introductory games, and because no real money is involved there are no age restrictions.

'One of the biggest predictors of whether people become gamblers is the playing of gambling-type games on free-play sites,' said Professor Griffiths, whose paper on adolescent gaming and gambling appears in the latest edition of the journal *Education and Health*.

'When you start winning, you start thinking that, if I was playing with real money, I could be doing quite well,' he said. 'Children who play these free games are more likely to gamble and more likely to develop problem gambling behaviours. These are gateway activities that can lead people down the gambling road.'

Professor Griffiths also insists that there is a significant overlap between gambling and seemingly innocuous online games. Many games allow players to customise their avatars by spending money on virtual accessories or extra clothing. 'It's a psychological masterstroke that people pay money to buy virtual items,' he said. 'The next step is for gambling firms to say, "Maybe you could win back some of the money you're spending."'

The immensely popular game Candy Crush Saga, which has been downloaded more than 500 million times, gives players the option of paying money to access higher levels.

'It's a bit like the old drug-dealing analogy of giving a bit for free and hooking them in,' Professor Griffiths said. 'Games like Candy Crush have a moreishness quality, a bit like chocolate. You say you'll just have one chunk and you end up having the whole lot. So you say, "I'll just play for 15 minutes", and you end up still there four or five hours later.'

In his paper for *Education and Health*, Professor Griffiths cites a 2011 study of more than 2,700 British secondary students, which found that 15 per cent had played free gambling games during the week prior to the survey. He writes that both gambling and social gaming offer intermittent, unpredictable rewards for users. The desire for such rewards draws the user into playing again and again.

Joe Hayman, chief executive of the UK's PSHE Association, agreed that gambling and Internet gaming could form part of Internet safety lessons. 'The big challenge is that PSHE has limited curriculum time in schools,' he said. 'Teachers have to choose which topics to cover. What they should be doing is identifying issues that are most pertinent to the lives of the young people at their schools, because they're not going to be able to cover everything.'

King, the company that makes Candy Crush Saga, insisted that its games were specifically targeted at adult women between the ages of 35 and 50, although the age range of players was currently widening. It added that it was possible to win the game without paying any money: at the moment, 40 per cent of players are paying users.

UK organisation Gamble Aware, which encourages responsible gambling, said that two per cent of people between the ages of 11 and 15 had trouble controlling their gambling behaviour. This was equivalent to 60,000 secondary students in Britain. 'Worryingly, those who begin their gambling careers earlier in life are more likely to be problem gamblers in adulthood,' the organisation stated.

10 January 2014

⇨ The above information is reprinted with kind permission from the *Times Educational Supplement*. Please visit www.tes.co.uk for further information.

What digital gambling is doing to Britain

The UK's 33,000 fixed-odds betting terminals each take almost £1,000 of punters' money per week. Welcome to 21st-century gambling...

Green Street, east London. I'm watching other people gamble at 10am on a Monday morning in a Ladbrokes betting shop. Virtual sports unfold on several screens: computer-generated horse and dog races, names every bit as daft as their flesh-and-blood counterparts (Boozy Beez, Gummy Bear, Mad Murphy).

But the real action is at the side of the shop where men hunch over the huge electronic machines: the fixed-odds betting terminals (FOBTs). Here, on virtual roulette games, vast amounts of people's money disappear every day. Each machine eats almost £1,000 a week.

Matt Zarb-Cousin, a 23-year-old from Essex, shows me how they work. Unlike the old fruit machines, there is no £2 cap per play. You can bet up to £100 every 20 seconds. Matt is a former FOBT addict who gave up three years ago after accumulating debts of £16,000.

'It must seem stupid but these machines can take over your life,' he says. 'Everything else in your life seems boring. Flat. My body would crave the quick, repetitive rush these things give you. If you lose you just think, okay this machine is taking me for a mug and I'm going to get some of my money back. And then you're chasing your losses. Again and again and again. And within 20 minutes you've lost £500.'

Matt is now campaigning with the group Stop the FOBTs to highlight the speed of losses on the high street ('it's casino gambling but five times as fast') and to try to force restrictions on the industry. It won't be easy. The profit generated by FOBTs has now reached more than £1.4bn a year. Approximately 50 per cent of the profits made by high-street bookies now come from the 33,000 FOBTs across Britain.

The Labour Party want tighter controls on the high-speed machines by increasing the time between bets and by giving councils the power to limit the number in each betting shop. The Prime Minister has said he'd rather wait for a key report later this year before taking any action.

Adrian Parkinson, formerly a senior manager at several national bookmakers, saw the impact on the industry as bosses began to understand the risk-free, profit-making potential of FOBTs. 'I hate these things,' he says. 'I absolutely hate what they've done. Betting was always about knowledge – knowing a lot about a horse to try to beat the bookmaker, the bookmaker changing the prices to cover potential losses, the punter trying to get the best of the prices.

'The machines have destroyed all that. You can't beat the FOBT. It's not about knowledge or skill. I saw how it draws a horrible addiction out in the ordinary punter who used to like a bet he could afford.'

Welcome to 21st-century gambling. Odds calculated by computer programs so companies can eliminate risk. Casino apps that let you throw money away on the bus home. Women in bed with their iPads losing thousands to online bingo. Ray Winstone popping up on TV to nod toward in-play flutters. Family finances wiped out without cash physically changing hands.

Problems cannot be completely hidden, however. Here in the east London borough of Newham (where there are 84 FOBT-happy bookmakers), councillors are concerned at how closely the borough crime map overlaps with the locations of betting shops. Matt Zarb-Cousin says relatively few incidents are actually reported, lest the bookies alert the authorities to the extent of the miserable, destructive rages FOBT losses can fuel.

'It's a weird culture,' he says. 'If I punched this machine and smashed the glass because I'd lost money, we could probably just walk out of here and nothing would happen. I saw it happen many times.'

Cowley, Oxford...

Owen Baily was a compulsive gambler for more than a decade. Today he works for Marks and Spencer and is 'enjoying normal life again'. He kicked his FOBTs habit last year following intense counselling sessions at a residential rehab centre. Owen's story raises some intriguing questions. What makes a gambler? Are some people prone to self-destruction? How much are they to blame for their own problems?

'My mum was a barmaid and from a young age I remember seeing the fruit machines as a fun thing to do,' says Owen. 'I actually met my dad – who was a compulsive gambler – for the very first time on Grand National Day, when I was 14 years old. He explained how form worked. It set something in stone. I saw gambling as the way I was going to earn my money.

'My dad spent a lot of time in casinos. When I was old enough, I began to go with him. I was excited by that environment. Cashiers handing over £25k, men in suits with crisp piles of notes. I wanted some of that. So I started playing roulette. It became my game. I won some but also lost lots of money. I was convinced I was good at it and tried to find a system for winning.'

The 'system' is one of gamblers' great delusions: a terrible trick they play on themselves. 'One of the other worst things that can happen is getting a big win,' says Owen. 'I once walked out of a casino with £5,500 shortly before Christmas. It felt great but it just fuelled my desire to go back.

'I lost everything and before long I couldn't cope with my job and I went into self-destruct with the FOBTs. I was homeless, had nothing. But if I could get a bit of money I'd be back on the FOBTs. I couldn't feel at ease until I was in front of that machine. It's like a magnet.'

But where does that underlying urge come from? 'It becomes so that you can't imagine life without it,' he says. 'If you take gambling away, what have I got in my life? No relationships, no interests. Really, under-lying everything, I was just very unhappy. I had a difficult upbringing and gambling became what I did to build myself up somehow – make myself a winner in life. Of course, it didn't work.

'At one point I realised I didn't like myself, didn't seem to care about myself or anyone else. I didn't give a f***. Underneath I was a very hurt child.'

Why is it that perfectly smart people keep doing something they know will make everything worse? Adrian Scarfe, a head consultant at the support organisation GamCare, tries to explain the nature of the addiction he helps treat. 'When you're hooked you can disassociate from the real world very easily and get locked into this cycle of anticipation, buzz, adrenalin rush. There is a release of serotonin and dopamine – they give you a high. When it's over, there is that flat feeling. It makes it damn difficult to stop.

Some people like risk. There is a competitive nature about individuals who like the idea of beating the odds, the bookmakers, the house. They feel the need to be seen as a winner – special. It's a complex thing. Some people actually come to like the loss because the loss confirms the underlying lack of self-worth. Freud thought gambling was an unconscious desire to fail.'

If we're bringing Freud into the equation, you might think this is not really a social problem. How can society regulate for stuff that belongs on therapists' couches? Yet the last British Gambling Prevalence Survey in 2010 showed that problem gambling in the UK had increased by 50 per cent in three years.

Like the FOBTs, the rise of online gambling – UK takings are thought to be £2 billion – is remarkable and worrying. The Internet has become the quickest and easiest outlet for the urge, and is ensnaring women at a faster rate than men. Half of all women callers to their helplines (up from 44 per cent on the previous year's figures) had problems with Internet gambling compared with a third of men.

Every week, new bingo and lotto sites arrive – awash in neon pink and fluffy animals – as the gaming industry tries to capitalise on the dressing-gown gambler market. Some offer tips on hosting 'online bingo parties', spurious guides to non-existent pyjama parties involving friends bringing round their laptops. The reality of web gaming is solitary, not social.

Vicky Clark's online addiction began with a 25p bet in May 2005, a Fantasy Five lotto game she saw as 'my little treat'. She soon moved from digital bingo to web casino games with higher stakes. Before long she was clicking for bets of £100 a time.

'Sometimes I'd win a few hundred pounds and it gave me such a buzz. But instead of stopping, I'd carry on and inevitably lose more. It didn't seem like real money, more like playing a game. I got caught up in the excitement of it.'

Vicky, 48, was forced to sell her Yorkshire hair-dressing business after accumulating £27,000 of debt. She now works in a hospital but was able to claim back £17,000 from one website that hadn't included all the necessary warnings. Vicky wants better player protection, with each person forced to set a total weekly spend at the point they register on a site. 'Why can't there be reasonable maximum limits?' she asks.

Shipbourne, Kent...

Justyn Larcombe is another recovering online gambler. The strange pull of betting websites took him by surprise and he remains shellshocked by how easily he lost it all. A former Army Major who served in Kosovo, Justyn was earning a six-figure salary as an insurance broker in the City of London.

'It's very weird because I hadn't placed a bet until I was 40 years old,' he explains. 'I was doing very, very well in financial services, lovely wife and children. I still wonder: where the hell did it come from? I think I was bored. I had started to work from home, felt a bit bored one day and put £5 on the rugby and unfortunately it won.

I thought, this is good this could be a little hobby. In the second year I began chasing my losses more frantically. By the third year I was hopelessly addicted to online casino stuff. At one point I worked out I had squandered £750,000 and had 15 different payday loans. I had to sell the house and by the time my wife had left me I was still selling the furniture.

'I was in a very low place. I think I could have killed myself if I hadn't been rescued, mostly by my family and faith. I got down on my knees and wept and admitted what I'd done to God and asked for help.'

But why? Why put so much at risk unnecessarily?

'I went from a high-pressure, high-adrenaline job to one where I could ease off a bit,' he says. 'So I probably needed some replacement for the buzz – some reassurance that I could get things right. It's that rush of controlling a lot of things at once. I was someone sought after in the City, puffed up with my own importance.

'Regardless of how much money you have, you want your importance constantly reaffirmed. Somehow I needed that again. Ending up with one bin liner and coming back to live at my mum's house, I was humiliated. I had to be humiliated to get rid of all that self-importance.

'It is a strange thing. Unfortunately, I think there is a trend with the digital stuff toward making this strange suspension of reality easier and easier, and it means the addiction will affect more people. That's a huge problem.'

You can't beat the (fixed odds) banker

⇨ Fixed-odds betting terminals (FOBTs) are touch-screen gaming machines found in betting shops across Britain. Bookies are limited to four FOBTs per shop.

⇨ British ex-bookmaker Steve Frater and Austrian computer whizz Walter Grubmuller invented FOBTs in Grubmuller's kitchen in the late 1990s. In 2006 they sold up to US giant Scientific Games Corporation for £104 million.

⇨ In 2001, first FOBT is introduced to the UK, by 2005 there are 20,000, and by 2013 there are 33,000 FOBTs in the UK.

⇨ You can bet £100 per spin every 20 seconds on casino games. The high-speed, high-stake nature of FOBT games has seen them dubbed the 'crack-cocaine of gambling'.

⇨ Annual profit generated for gambling industry: £1.4 billion (50% of all profits made by land-based bookmakers).

⇨ The industry claims FOBTs have an average payout of 97% but this is based on each spin. Each spin sees payout degradation (£100 x 97% becomes £97 x 97% becomes £94.09 x 97%, etc.).

⇨ £8,567,000 is the amount lost by gamblers using FOBTs in Bethnal Green and Bow in 2012.

27 February 2014

⇨ The above information is reprinted with kind permission from *The Big Issue*. Please visit www.bigissue.com for further information.

Can gambling be useful? You bet

Incorporate risk and uncertain outcomes into lessons and you'll be on to a winner, Darren Evans writes.

From furtive games of pitch-and-toss in the playground to friendly bets on a classmate's sporting prowess, gambling games have always been played by children in school. But can gambling, or gaming, with its associated and usually negative elements of risk-taking and instant gratification, ever be used in a positive and constructive way to motivate learning in the classroom?

It is a question that has prompted groundbreaking research by a team of neuroscientists at the University of Bristol, who set out to investigate the links between games, brains and learning.

'We wanted to find out why games educated us,' says Paul Howard-Jones, who led the research. 'It has a lot to do with the attraction of uncertain reward.'

The key is a chemical called dopamine, which is associated with the brain's reward system and creates feelings of enjoyment. It can motivate a person to perform certain activities, plays an important role in behaviour and is usually associated with rewarding experiences, such as eating or having sex.

'Research on the brains of monkeys shows that there is an increased level of dopamine transmission in the mid-brain when a reward is likely, and that is enhanced by the uncertainty of the reward,' Dr Howard-Jones says.

'Uncertain reward is present in everyday life in so many circumstances – going for an interview, for example. It's a very important part of what keeps us motivated in life.

'School is the only place where you have an artificially maintained reward relationship. The traditional approach to motivation in the classroom is that if you have the correct answer, you should be given a reward. There's a sense of social justice about that. Neuroscience says something different; that to get people motivated, you should offer them the chance of getting a reward.'

The research has resulted in the creation of Zondle Team Play, a unique piece of software that allows teachers to use a different approach to teaching by turning any lesson into a game.

Pupils are split into teams to answer multiple-choice questions. The teacher sets the topic and allocates the number of points available for each question. She goes through the possible answers in order and asks each team to choose one. The teams are then given the choice to gamble, or 'game', their score by opting to double or zero it on a 'wheel of chance'.

Raising the stakes

Once the correct answer is revealed, the teams who got it right but did not 'game' are allocated points, while those who answered correctly but chose to 'game' wait for their turn on the wheel. If it stops spinning on a blue strip they are allocated double points. If it stops on a white one, they get no points.

According to researchers, the pupils' emotional response to a lesson was more positive and engaged when the gaming element was introduced.

'It's important to have the emotional ups and downs in the classroom because we know it can provoke memory formation,' Dr Howard-Jones explains. 'Putting an element of uncertainty into the academic tests allows children to experience more of those emotional highs and lows. In a game context, the chance of success is 50-50 and that's when you get the best dopamine response.

'Those are the moments children are going to remember. All eyes are on the board. There's a tense silence. You have their attention and you can explain why the other answers are incorrect.'

At the point before the wheel of chance is spun, the rising anticipation helps to create a 'teachable moment' where the teacher can provide feedback and explanation and the learning can be embedded.

Dr Howard-Jones believes the research has huge potential but acknowledges that it is still early days. Although the researchers have yet to carry out large-scale randomised, controlled trials of the methodology to scientifically gauge its effectiveness, they have already had plenty of positive feedback from schools.

Dawn Hallybone, ICT coordinator at Oakdale Junior School in London, has been using Team Play in history, maths and science with Years 5 and 6 (P5/6) since last summer. She finds the game useful to introduce new topics or for revision purposes, and says the response from pupils is 'amazing'.

'We use a lot of game-based learning in school but the reaction to Team Play is really interesting,' she says. 'They feel as if they are on a television show and take it really seriously. You see them start to devise strategies; at first, everyone wants to double their score all the time, but eventually they only choose to double if they are certain the answer is correct.

'They start talking to each other about the topic and you find them arguing the case for their answers. They are keen to learn more, and as a teacher it's important to recognise the point at which they are most engaged and to capitalise on that to embed the learning.'

Dr Howard-Jones says that when one Year 9 (S2) science class in England used the technique over a series of lessons, the majority of pupils said they would prefer to learn that way all the time.

'It often leads to more motivational discourse,' he says. 'You hear a lot of sporting talk from pupils who would never normally speak like that. For example, if they are doing badly they blame it on bad luck, but if they are doing well it is because of their skill.

'Less able children often win and the most able children do not always win. But it doesn't seem to put off the most able.

'One of the first questions we had was whether introducing chance into the learning environment would reduce fairness. We tested this with a group of Year 9 science pupils, using a vicious game in which rolling a dice in the wrong way could take away all the points they had accumulated over the past 20 minutes. We thought they would be in uproar but they thought it was fantastic.'

Mark Griffiths, director of the International Gaming Research Unit at Nottingham Trent University, who has spent 26 years researching gambling, says that utilising the fun and competitive element of gambling can be motivational in the classroom.

'You are using the word "gamble" without any financial meaning whatsoever and there's no evidence that would have a harmful effect,' he says. 'Plus it's being done in the safe environment of the classroom. I can see nothing wrong in using (gambling's) mechanisms in a safe environment to motivate children's learning in this way.'

No money changes hands in the gambling games in the classroom. It is the notion of risk and chance that boosts the educational effect, they say.

Up for debate

An unexpected supporter of the approach is Adrian Scarfe, head of clinical training at GamCare, a charity that wants more information and education about gambling in the classroom.

GamCare made national newspaper headlines in 2011 for its campaign to educate children about gambling alongside such topics as sex, drugs and alcohol abuse in personal, social and health education (PSHE) lessons.

Dr Scarfe believes that introducing gambling through the Team Play lesson structure could be useful in linking to a discussion later on the wider issue of gambling and its risks.

'This seems to be a very good and creative teaching technique that would aid the learning process,' he says. 'And teachers could expand on it to approach the subject of gambling and the processes involved in more detail.'

He believes it is critical that teachers understand gambling, and are able to talk about responsible and irresponsible forms. 'Within the topic of gambling is a whole range of positive lessons for pupils – how to manage risk and reward, how to manage resources and understand personal finance, calculating probability, even its impact on health and social life,' he says.

Researcher Mark Griffiths agrees. He has helped to produce a number of free resources for schools on gambling, including exercises looking at perceptions of the activity and its potential risks. But these also flag up the fact that it can be sensibly enjoyed by adults.

'This is something that does need to be taught more formally in schools, because we know prevention is better than cure,' he says.

A game of chance

Despite the elements of chance and risk inherent in the Team Play game, Dr Howard-Jones refutes suggestions that the lessons could lead to further gambling by pupils.

'There is no research linking teaching through gaming to producing gambling behaviour,' Dr Howard-Jones explains. 'The reason why we have pursued this particular avenue is because we have found it to be helpful in understanding the attraction of video games, which usually do not involve any monetary gain.

'We are not offering any material rewards of any particular value. This is not about purely chance, but chance and how it relates to learning.'

22 February 2013

⇨ The above information is reprinted with kind permission from the *Times Education Supplement*. Please visit www.tes.co.uk for further information.

Are students turning to gambling in the face of increased money troubles?

By Jess Denham

One in five students are turning to gambling as a way to make money at university, while one in four would consider selling their body to medical trials or the adult entertainment industry.

Leading student money website Save the Student carried out a nationwide survey on over 2,300 undergrads to assess the impact that financial worries are having on the student population. Findings released this week show that nearly 80% of current students are concerned about having enough money to live on, claiming that their academic studies and diet suffers due to a lack of funds.

Along with high tuition fees and rising living costs, rental prices have increased considerably in recent years, forcing the average student to halve their spending on 'luxuries' such as socialising and clothes. While many seek a part-time job to try and alleviate money troubles this restricts the amount of time they can spend on degree commitments, adding to already building stress and anxiety levels. As a result, students begin to consider alternative means of raising funds, leading them into addictive habits and potentially dangerous situations.

Thomas, 23, an economics student at Nottingham, began playing poker when he turned 18. Sharing his experience he explained: 'I came to see poker as a part-time job at university. My friends gambled a bit here and there, but mainly for a laugh – their livelihoods were not dependent on it. For me, a session online would last anywhere between 18 and 36 hours and I would do at least five a month. I spent a lot of my winnings on drinks and bought myself a BMW for my 21st. The main thing though is that I can now afford to take a Maths PGCE without having to apply for yet another loan.

'I was called anti-social once or twice but I never saw it as a risk. Swings of losses and wins happen but it's about the bigger picture - as long as the overall trend is up it's okay. I once lost close to £4,000 in 14 hours but in my best session I won close to £11,000 in 22. I am looking forward to entering the working world but this is a job that fitted into my student lifestyle at a time when I needed funds.'

Ed Pinkney, founder of student mental health charity Mental Wealth UK, said: 'As a recent survey from National Union of Students shows, many students are feeling desperate. There is a strong link between financial difficulties and mental health issues and the Government ought to be closely monitoring the effect on young people of increased tuition fees and a tough jobs market.'

As for medical trials, offering yourself as a human guinea pig for drugs that have yet to be used on humans is a risky business. Sure the horror stories are, in reality, rare, but side effects such as headaches, lethargy and nausea are common and many may not be experienced until years later.

Christian, 21, a student at Nottingham Trent, registered for a medical trial in a bid to relieve money worries. "It involved two visits to a hospital in Nottingham where I was fed through a tube down my nose and underwent a scan. The doctors were investigating the best practice for feeding ill patients. I was really hard up at the time – it was third year and the cost of travelling for my dissertation had taken its toll. This offered me a chance to make £160 in ten hours. I was friends with a medic who suggested it so I felt safer and couldn't see any immediate danger to my health. It was an uncomfortable experience but at the time it was either that or going further into my overdraft."

So what can be done to discourage students from risking their mental and physical well-being in the pursuit of funds? Jake Butler, editor of *Save the Student*, commented: 'It's clear that now, more than ever before, students require much more in the way of support, awareness and wider education when it comes to personal finance. It really does concern me when we see how much worry and stress money issues are causing, when after all students should be focusing 100% on their studies.'

4 June 2013

⇨ The above information is reprinted with kind permission from *The Independent*. Please visit www.independent.co.uk for further information.

Teenage kicks

It was about a year ago that I realised gambling was seriously affecting my home life so I did what all self-respecting gamblers would do.

I stopped going home.

Once gambling is in your blood, like herpes it's there to stay.

Indulge too much in drugs and one day soon you'll end up dead. Likewise alcohol. But an addiction to gambling is pretty much limitless.

Your liver doesn't give up on you. Or your heart. The only thing that usually dries up quick is the money, and there are always other sources for that.

A documentary on Channel 4 a few years ago (it was called *Teenage Gamblers*) showed the damage done to the family with two young sons hooked on fruit machines.

When their own pocket money dried up there was always mum's purse, always something to pawn (by the looks of the gargantuan mum, always something to eat too). The hour-long documentary stopped short of telling us there was always something to steal, but we knew that was the logical next step.

We were meant to shake our heads in despair that the liberal gambling laws ushered in by the last Labour Government are breeding an underclass of teenage gambling desperadoes, but somewhere during the hour of that programme, I recall, a different story emerged.

Matthew, just 18, had inherited his instinct to gamble from his father Dave, a lifelong punter. He had also inherited a certain canniness, an understanding of odds that you suspect will stand him in good stead in betting's twilight world.

Dad Dave felt no shame that he had bred and tutored a gambling nut. In fact there was an undisguised pride in the betting maturity of his son. And no wonder.

'People say gambling is a sin,' said Matthew, 'but wouldn't it be a bigger sin to go out drinking and kick someone's head in?'

He went on: 'A lot of people my age try to persuade me to go clubbing but I find it pointless. You go out, have a few drinks, don't really speak properly, don't remember what happens. You wake up next morning with a headache and you've spent a hundred quid. What's the point of that? Go to a casino with £100 and you're trying to turn it into £100,000. There's a point to it.'

There was no hint of desperation in Matthew's approach to gambling, even though he spent his 18th birthday playing 12 straight hours of blackjack. It's in his blood, he knows he will bet until he dies, yet not only does he have it under control, he shows every sign of being able to make the game pay.

And that's the perfect answer to all the doom-mongers who fear Britain is going to hell in a handcart, pushed there by a gigantic wave of new-born gambling addicts. Drug addiction is bad news. So too alcohol addiction. But gambling addiction is ruinous only if you lose. Who's to say gambling addicts can't win?

Why should we wring our hands about teenage gamblers? I'd bet every single one of you reading this was a committed gambler by the time you were 15. Those whose hobby subsequently developed into a damaging addiction have my sympathy but the odds are you'd have ended up that way even if you had not struck your first bet until you were 21.

I have two sons and when they're 15 I hope they're up early studying form instead of wasting their lives in the half-man/half-mattress world of the normal teenager.

When I was 15 – that awkward age between hopscotch and real Scotch – I wrote a sex manual for teenagers. It read: 'In. Out. Repeat if necessary.' I also bet. Almost every day. My dad was manager of a betting shop and he taught me to avoid the kind of mug bets that helped pay his wages.

He showed me the best races to bet each-way. The trainers to follow at certain courses. How to count from two to king. I'm not saying I was clued up but everyone in my class in school in 1974 was told two weeks beforehand that 50-1 outsider Snow Knight would win that year's Derby.

What I'm saying is that I had the perfect pedigree to be a hopelessly addicted gambler but developed only into a largely hopeless gambler, with no sign of addiction. Why should other teenage gamblers be any different?

But if Britain truly is worried about spawning a nation of teenage betting zombies, perhaps the salutary tale of Philip Tilson should be dusted off and given another airing.

Tilson was the poor guy who in 1993 thought he'd won more that £100,000 from Ladbrokes but ended up with precisely nothing after Ladbrokes, following a long-running and highly acrimonious dispute, were tipped off that Tilson was only 17 years old and therefore not able legally to place a bet.

Though Ladbrokes, in paying Tilson nothing, were adhering to the strict letter of the law, they risked opening an enormous can of worms.

In arguing that as Tilson was under 18 (the minimum legal age to bet) they were within their rights to pay him zilch, Ladbrokes begged one obvious question: If under-18s are not allowed to win money from gambling, is it right that they are allowed to lose?

Let's all of us go to Ladbrokes and demand a refund on all those losers we backed before we were 18.

4 October 2013

Study highlights need for more social responsibility by online gaming industry

Online game companies need to be more socially responsible for over-addictive use of their products to avoid government intervention, according to a new study by academics from Nottingham Trent, Cardiff and Derby universities.

The study, in the journal *Addiction Research and Theory*, was led by Dr Shumaila Yousafzai of Cardiff Business School with psychologists Professor Mark Griffiths from Nottingham Trent University and Dr Zaheer Hussain from the University of Derby.

While conventional videogames have an ending, or may become boring and repetitive, Massively Multiplayer Online Role Playing Games (MMORPGs) are an inexhaustible system of goals and success, in which the character becomes stronger and richer by moving to new levels while accumulating treasures, power and weaponry.

In recent years, the problematic use of online videogames has received increased attention not only from the media, but also from psychologists, psychiatrists, mental health organisations and gamers themselves.

A number of studies from different cultures are providing evidence that somewhere around seven to 11% of gamers seem to be having real problems to the point that they are considered pathological gamers. Some are reported to have been playing for 40, 60, and even near 90 hours in a gaming session.

Professor Mark Griffiths said: 'The proportion of gamers who develop problems and/or become addicts may stay roughly constant but as online games get better and better, and increasing numbers of people discover them, the number of addicts is most probably going to rise.

'We therefore propose to proactively approach the main online game publishers and explore options for collaboration between academics, healthcare, and the video game industry in order to provide proper referral, customer care, and information to the general public.'

Dr Yousafzai said: 'The warning messages on the loading screens of popular online videogames raise the question of why the online videogame industry warns its players not to overuse their product. Does the videogame industry really believe that their products have addictive features that can lead to negative consequences and the functional impairment of gamers' lives?

These warning messages also suggest that the online videogame industry might know how high the percentage of over-users is, how much time gamers' spend playing, and what specific features makes a particular game more engrossing and addictive than others. While they do not directly admit this, by showing the warning messages, they do take some responsibility into their own hands.'

Dr Hussain said: 'Online game developers are already working on bringing Online Role Playing Games to consoles. This type of game is most often implicated in cases of online game overuse and, as console systems have more market share than PCs, the number of 'videogame addicts' will increase in the coming time.

'Our study found that although warning messages about risk of overuse have recently started to appear on the loading screens of popular MMORPGs, this is not enough.

'Previous research has suggested that responsible game operators can try to help gamers improve control over their own behaviour by following a three-step strategy of combining good game design with effective gamers' care polices, and referral services.

'As a first step, online game developers and publishers need to look into the structural features of the game design; for example, the character development, rapid absorption rate, and multi-player features which could make them addictive and/or problematic for some gamers. One idea could be to shorten long quests to minimise the time spent in the game obtaining a certain prized item.'

The universities' study warns that if game companies refuse to create restraints for players, and their games grow in greater popularity, then Western governments may have no choice but to follow in the steps of their Asian counterparts, who have already taken steps to reduce the potentially problematic effects of game play by limiting usage.

6 August 2013

⇨ The above information is reprinted with kind permission from Nottingham Trent University. Please visit www.ntu.ac.uk for further information.

Study refutes claims that bookies prey on the poor

A new independent report has undermined allegations that high street bookmakers target deprived areas and vulnerable people. It comes as Prime Minister David Cameron prepares to announce measures to curb gaming machines, reacting to concerns about the social cost of the machines.

The report, carried out by the Local Data Company, reveals that just 17% of Britain's betting shops are in the most deprived areas of the country, compared to 35% in the least deprived areas. In total, almost two-thirds (62%) of betting shops are in areas with lower than average levels of deprivation.

Matthew Hopkinson, director of the Local Data Company, commented: 'It is clear that betting shops are not clustered in towns with high deprivation scores. A minority of shops are in the poorest areas, while a majority are in the least deprived areas.'

Key findings are:

⇨ Areas with highest levels of deprivation have the lowest number of betting shops (17%), while least deprived areas have the most (35%)

⇨ New shop openings over past three years concentrated in Britain's least deprived areas

⇨ Shops in the most deprived areas are less profitable for bookies compared to least deprived areas

⇨ Number of betting shops increased by just 1.3% in 2013 – showing proliferation of high street bookmakers is much slower than widely believed.

In addition, the report finds no evidence that the industry targets the poorest people. Analysis of town populations, split by socio-economic group, shows no difference per head of population between the number of betting shops in ABC1 areas and the number in C2DE areas.

Hopkinson explained: 'There is nothing in the data to suggest that bookmakers deliberately target poor and vulnerable people. Our analysis shows new shop openings are primarily in towns with low and average deprivation scores – not in the poorest areas.'

The report also reveals the expansion in the number of high street bookmakers is much less aggressive than has been widely reported. In 2013, the number of shops increased by just 1.3%, compared to growth rates of over 3% in the number of pawnbrokers, coffee shops and convenience stores on British high streets. In total, bookies account for just 1.7% of all live retail units in Britain.

An analysis of closures and new openings in the three years up to December 2013 reveals new shop openings have been concentrated in Britain's least deprived areas.

The findings of the report also appear to discredit claims that shops in deprived areas are the most profitable, which critics say has led to the industry targeting poor areas. An analysis of gross win data per shop per capita illustrates that shops in the poorest areas are not as profitable as shops in areas with lower levels of deprivation – clearly suggesting there is no commercial incentive for bookmakers to target poorer areas.

Dirk Vennix, Chief Executive of the Association of British Bookmakers, said: 'The betting industry does not target the poor and the vulnerable. It never has, and it never will. This report should help dispel some damaging myths propagated by those trying to demonise and toxify our industry.

'We are a responsible and regulated industry selling a mainstream leisure product enjoyed by over eight million people per year. We choose where to locate our shops in the same way as any other retailer would – using commercial factors such as consumer demand, footfall and competitive presence. It makes no sense whatsoever for us to target poor communities or vulnerable people.'

14 April 2014

⇨ The above information is reprinted with kind permission from SBC News. Please visit www.sbcnews. co.uk for further information.

High-stakes gambling machines 'suck money from poorest communities'

MPs express alarm about £5 billion spent on fixed odds betting terminals in northern cities and London boroughs.

By Randeep Ramesh

More than £5 billion was gambled on high-speed, high-stakes gambling machines in northern England cities and London boroughs with high levels of unemployment last year – four times the amount bet in richer rural areas in southern England where jobless numbers are low, according to an analysis for *The Guardian*.

The report reveals that in the 50 parliamentary constituencies with the highest numbers of unemployed people, punters visited 1,251 betting shops and put £5.6 billion into 4,454 so-called fixed odds betting terminals (FOBTs). By comparison, the 50 constituencies with the lowest levels of unemployment had only 287 betting shops and 1,045 terminals, and saw £1.4 billion gambled last year.

The figures, produced for Fairer Gambling – a non-profit organisation which campaigns against problem betting, run by a gambling expert who helped bring the casino-style fixed odds machines to the UK high street – appear to show that bookmakers have deliberately targeted the poorest areas with the highest unemployment and poverty. It is a charge the industry vigorously rejects.

In east London's Bethnal Green and Bow, the 45 betting shops saw £243 million placed in bets on machines, dubbed the 'crack cocaine of gambling', which offer quickfire casino games allowing players to stake up to £100 on a 20-second spin of the wheel. Punters can play with cash, or pay with credit or debit cards at the counter. By comparison, in Oxfordshire's Henley not a single licence had been issued for a betting shop.

Lucy Powell, Labour MP for Manchester Central, said she was shocked that £190 million was being gambled in her local area. 'There are mind-numbing numbers of betting shops in places like Moston in my constituency. I think it is a moral question to ask whether it is a good thing that betting companies are targeting the poor and whether government lets them.

'According to these figures, there's more being spent on gambling than by the council in my constituency on services.'

The profit made by betting shops, known as the gross gambling yield, in the 50 poorest constituencies was just over £173 million, according to the Campaign for Fairer Gambling, which gleaned the figures from analysis of industry data.

There appears a distinctive political divide, with the betting shops clustered in Labour MPs' constituencies and almost absent in Tory MPs' backyards. Diane Abbott, MP for Hackney North and Stoke Newington, said almost £200 million was spent on betting in her constituency last year. 'It's a business model which sucks money from the poorest communities,' she said, adding that hundreds of public order offences were committed outside betting shops every week, contributing to low-level social disorder.

However, Tories blamed the culture of poor people rather than betting companies for exploiting them. John Redwood, the Conservative MP for Wokingham in Berkshire, which has three betting shops, said he had been surprised by the spread of bookmakers in poorer areas.

'I put it down to the fact that poor people believe there's one shot to

get rich. They put getting rich down to luck and think they can take a gamble,' he said.

'They also have time on their hands. My voters are too busy working hard to make a reasonable income.'

At the heart of the debate is whether the Government should intervene to reshape the nation's high streets. Last July, the culture media and sport select committee called for the lifting of the limited number of high-stakes gambling machines allowed in each betting shop. Currently, bookmakers are limited to four machines per shop. The machines are hugely lucrative, bringing in on average £900 a week in profits, so bookmakers have bypassed the restriction by opening more branches in high streets – 'clustering' in poorer areas.

However, Labour said the select committee was wrong, and instead the opposition agreed with Mary Portas, the retail guru, who argued in her government review that 'the influx of betting shops, often in more deprived areas, is blighting our high streets'. Her analysis was that betting shops were cluttering up Britain because they were listed as 'financial services' in planning guidelines.

This meant empty shopfronts that once contained banks and building societies could be converted into betting shops without any planning permission. The Portas retail review urged ministers to remove this anomaly and instead ensure every prospective bookmaker would have to apply for planning permission.

Hilary Benn, the shadow local government spokesman whose Leeds central constituency saw £132 million gambled last year, said: 'There should be a separate use class order for betting shops under planning rules so that local communities and councils can decide how many shops they wish to have in their area. This will help deal with the problem of clustering. I do not support a relaxation of the current limit on the number of high-value machines.'

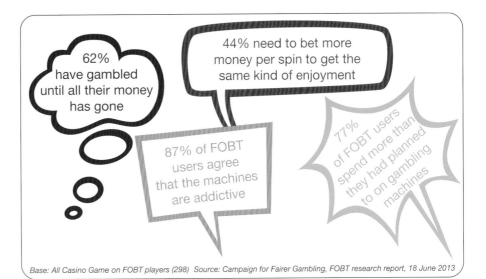

62% have gambled until all their money has gone

44% need to bet more money per spin to get the same kind of enjoyment

87% of FOBT users agree that the machines are addictive

77% of FOBT users spend more than they had planned to on gambling machines

Base: All Casino Game on FOBT players (298) Source: Campaign for Fairer Gambling, FOBT research report, 18 June 2013

Adrian Parkinson, who worked for the Tote, was involved with launching fixed-odds betting terminals from 1999 until 2008, and authored the study for the Campaign for Fairer Gambling. He said: 'Despite what the bookmakers and their supportive MPs say, the proliferation of betting shops is driven by FOBTs, and is focused on the most deprived areas in the UK.'

He argued that the culture secretary already had the power to rein in the bookmakers. 'The Gambling Act 2005 gives Maria Miller the power to reduce the maximum stake and increase the time between spins without primary legislation, so there is no excuse for government inaction.'

In a statement, the Association of British Bookmakers (ABB) said: 'The idea that bookmakers target vulnerable communities is both false and offensive. Like any other retailer, we locate our shops where footfall is high and rents are affordable. These factors vary, which explains there can be different numbers of shops in different parts of the country.

'At a time of economic uncertainty and record retail vacancies, we are proud to play our part in supporting jobs right across the UK.'

Bookmakers claim that the Campaign for Fairer Gambling is motivated by commercial interests. The Campaign for Fairer Gambling was founded by Derek Webb, founder of casino games developer Prime Table Games, which he sold in October last year to the Las Vegas-based Galaxy Gaming for $23 million (£15 million). Webb and his partner Hannah O'Donnell took the payment as $800,000 in Galaxy shares and the rest in two promissory notes.

The ABB said: 'Betting shops have been located on our nation's high streets ever since off-course betting was first made legal in 1961. The betting industry would welcome an evidence-based debate, but the research presented is misleading. Fairer Gambling is an organisation with a commercial interest in running down high street bookies. This inaccurate piece of research discredits their place in this debate.'

The Government said it was reviewing fixed-odd betting terminals and would respond to the select committee 'within weeks'. A Department for Culture, Media & Sport spokesman said: 'We will undertake a review of the evidence around fixed-odds betting terminals and problem gambling. An announcement about the scope and timing of the review will be made in due course.'

4 January 2013

⇨ The above information is reprinted with kind permission from *The Guardian*. Please visit www.theguardian.com for further information.

Chapter 2

New study reveals scale of problem gambling among homeless population

Homeless people are ten times more likely to be problem gamblers than the UK population as a whole, researchers at Cambridge have found.

The study – one of the largest surveys of gambling and homelessness ever undertaken in the UK – provides new insight into a rarely studied problem and suggests homeless services should offer clients more support to identify and tackle problem gambling.

Although homelessness and problem gambling are two public health concerns, they are rarely considered together. This new study – published in the *Journal of Gambling Studies* – interviewed 450 people at homeless hostels and shelters in the London Borough of Westminster.

According to lead author Steve Sharman from the Department of Psychology: 'Many issues face the homeless population, including drug and alcohol use. In terms of addiction research, most focus has been on drugs, alcohol and smoking, but the gambling field is relatively small in comparison. And while it is possible to spot physiological indicators of drug and alcohol addiction, problem gambling is much harder to identify.

Finding out more about gambling addiction is important at a time when gambling opportunities are wider than ever. 'Gambling has exploded in popularity over the past 20 years, partly due to changes in legislation but also because of new technology,' said Sharman.

'Where previous generations were limited to betting shops and football pools, today there's everything from online slots to in-play betting. That means people can gamble 24 hours a day, seven days a week, and the more people who gamble, the more people there will be who do so problematically.'

Together with researchers at Kings College London, the National Problem Gambling Clinic, The Connection @ St Martins and other centres in Westminster, Sharman spoke to over 450 homeless people in London.

He assessed levels of problem gambling using a standard clinical diagnostic tool called the Problem Gambling Severity Index. He then compared the results with data from the British Gambling Prevalence Survey.

Compared with the UK population as a whole, where problem gambling affects 0.7% of people, the level of problem gambling among homeless people was 11.6%. 'We found that the rate of problem or pathological gambling is significantly higher in the homeless population than the general population,' he said.

In identifying the significant scale of the problem, the study could pave the way to developing new services for the homeless.

'The results are useful because some homeless services don't ask about gambling in their initial assessments. By showing that this population is vulnerable to gambling addiction, the study should encourage homeless services to include questions about gambling in their assessments. If they can understand the full range of behavioural problems their clients face – not only substance abuse – then they will be able to provide more comprehensive services,' said Sharman.

The next stage of the project will be to unpick the direction of the link between gambling and homelessness – whether gambling is a cause or consequence of homelessness – the links between gambling and alcohol and drug use, and look at so-called negative life events.

'By giving us an indication of life events that precede homelessness and came afterwards, we will get a better understanding of the causes, and whether people start gambling after becoming homeless or became homeless as a result of gambling,' he said.

'Regardless of whether gambling is a cause or a consequence, recognising and addressing this problem will hopefully give affected individuals a better chance of getting off – and more importantly staying off – the streets.'

2 April 2014

⇨ The above information is reprinted with kind permission from the University of Cambridge. Please visit www.cam.ac.uk for further information.

Problem gambling

‘Problem gambling is gambling to a degree that compromises, disrupts or damages family, personal or recreational pursuits’ (National Centre for Social Research).

Problematic gambling is seen as an 'invisible addiction', unlike other forms of addiction there are no visible signs, e.g. physical deterioration. Many gamblers hide their gambling from family and friends. If you have a problem with your gambling pattern, it may start or already be affecting your family life, relationships, finances, work or emotional well-being.

Gambling behaviour exists on a continuum with extreme pathological gambling, presenting major disruption to the individual and wider community, and to Social Gambling, presenting no problems. Gamblers can move in and out of problematic stages of gambling throughout their gambling life.

Here are some common signs of problem gambling:

⇨ The person gambles more than they intended

⇨ Other people are suggesting that the person might have a gambling problem

⇨ The person is feeling guilty about the way he or she gambles

⇨ The person wants to stop betting money and feels as if they can't

⇨ The person gambling is hiding betting slips, lottery tickets, gambling money or other signs of betting

⇨ There are arguments over how the person gambling is handling money

⇨ The person gambling is borrowing money and not repaying it

⇨ The person gambling is losing time from work or school due to gambling.

Additional signs of problem gambling include:

⇨ Preoccupation with gambling (reliving past gambling experiences, planning the next venture or thinking of ways in which to gamble)

⇨ Needing to gamble with increasing amounts of money in order to achieve the desired excitement

⇨ Trying to control, cut down or stop gambling unsuccessfully

⇨ Feeling restless or irritable when attempting to cut down or stop gambling

⇨ Using gambling as a way to escape problems or bad moods (helplessness, guilt, anxiety, depression)

⇨ Returning to gambling after losing money gambling

⇨ Lying to conceal the extent of involvement with gambling

⇨ Committing illegal acts, such as forgery, fraud, theft or embezzlement to finance gambling

⇨ Jeopardising or losing a significant relationship, job, educational or career opportunity because of gambling

⇨ Relying on others to get out of debt (bailouts).

Source: The American Psychiatric Association's Diagnostic Statistical Manual of Mental Disorders(DSM-IV)

⇨ The above information is reprinted with kind permission from Aquarius. Please visit www.aquarius.org.uk for further information.

Risks of gambling

Although it may not seem as destructive as the effects of drugs or alcohol, gambling can impact on many aspects of your life including family and relationships, your finances, your work and even your health.

Family and relationships

Problem gamblers spend more time gambling or thinking about gambling and it can become extremely difficult to maintain a normal family life. This creates stress and has a negative impact on relationships and family life.

⇨ Families usually have more arguments over money and get hounded by debt collectors.

⇨ Problem gamblers might miss family activities, including meals, birthdays and other important events.

⇨ 'Casino kids' sometimes are left in cars at gambling venues while a parent bets.

⇨ Increased arguments within the family.

⇨ Compulsive gamblers more often provoke reactive violence in their spouses.

⇨ Children of problem gamblers typically have lower grades, higher substance abuse rates and more frequent suicide attempts.

⇨ Children of problem gamblers could be more likely to develop gambling problems themselves.

⇨ Problem gamblers are more likely to become separated or divorced.

Financial risk

Problem gamblers' finances will fluctuate from time to time as they experience periods when they win regularly but also experience high levels of loss. Although a problem gambler may occasionally experience 'big wins' they should also expect to see an increase in financial difficulties.

⇨ Increasing debts.

⇨ 'Maxed out' credit cards.

⇨ Overdue utility bills, which might result in cut-offs.

⇨ Borrowing from family and friends.

⇨ Pawning personal and family valuables.

⇨ Passing bad cheques.

⇨ Eviction and forced home sales.

⇨ Bankruptcy.

Problem gamblers are more likely to commit crimes to support their habits. This can include tax evasion, cheque forgery, stealing credit cards, fraudulent loan applications, insurance fraud, theft, embezzlement, fencing stolen goods, unlicensed bookmaking, arson and even armed robbery.

Health risks

Most people may not see a connection between their gambling and their health; however, problem gambling is associated with a range of emotional, physical and psychological health problems.

⇨ Self-esteem declines as losses increase.

⇨ Problem gamblers suffer more from stress, anxiety, moodiness, attention deficit hyperactivity, obsessive-compulsive disorders and manic and clinical depression.

⇨ Some physical problems experienced by problem gamblers include muscular tension, fatigue, stomach ailments, insomnia, colitis, high blood pressure, heart disease, migraines and skin problems.

⇨ Problem gamblers are likely to use alcohol, cigarettes or other drugs to cope with the guilt or desperate situation.

⇨ High proportions of problem gamblers seriously consider or even attempt suicide.

⇨ Problem gamblers are more likely to smoke.

Job risk

⇨ Problem gambling can also have an adverse effect on an individual's ability to perform well at work, college or school.

⇨ Problem gamblers often show up late for work.

⇨ Some problem gamblers skip entire work days to gamble.

⇨ They are more likely to take sick leave.

⇨ Problem gamblers usually experience decreased productivity, as they often daydream about gambling or use the Internet at work to gamble.

⇨ They are more likely to ask employers for pay advances, borrow money from fellow employees, steal from work and embezzle.

⇨ There is a real risk of losing your job due to your gambling behaviour due to high levels of sickness, absenteeism and misuse of company time.

⇨ The above information is reprinted with kind permission from Aquarius. Please visit www.aquarius.org.uk for further information.

Understanding gambling addiction and problem gambling

Gambling addiction, also known as compulsive gambling, is a type of impulse-control disorder. Compulsive gamblers can't control the impulse to gamble, even when they know their gambling is hurting themselves or their loved ones. Gambling is all they can think about and all they want to do, no matter the consequences. Compulsive gamblers keep gambling whether they're up or down, broke or flush, happy or depressed. Even when they know the odds are against them, even when they can't afford to lose, people with a gambling addiction can't 'stay off the bet'.

Gamblers can have a problem, however, without being totally out of control. Problem gambling is any gambling behaviour that disrupts your life. If you're preoccupied with gambling, spending more and more time and money on it, chasing losses or gambling despite serious consequences, you have a gambling problem.

Relieving unpleasant and overwhelming feelings without gambling

Unpleasant feelings such as stress, depression, loneliness, fear and anxiety can trigger compulsive gambling or make it worse. After a stressful day at work, after an argument with your spouse or coworker, or to avoid more time spent on your own, an evening at the track or the casino can seem like a fun, exciting way to unwind and socialise. But there are healthier and far less expensive ways to keep unpleasant feelings in check. These may include exercising, meditating, spending time with friends, taking up new hobbies or exploring relaxation techniques.

For many people, an important aspect of quitting gambling is to find alternate ways to handle these difficult feelings without gambling. Even when gambling is no longer a part of your life, the painful and unpleasant feelings that may have prompted you to gamble in the past will still remain. So, it's worth spending some time thinking about the different ways you intend to deal with stressful situations and the daily irritations that would normally trigger you to start gambling.

Signs and symptoms of problem gambling

Gambling addiction is sometimes referred to as the 'hidden illness' because there are no obvious physical signs or symptoms like there are in drug or alcohol addiction. Problem gamblers typically deny or minimise the problem. They also go to great lengths to hide their gambling. For example, problem gamblers often withdraw from their loved ones, sneak around, and lie about where they've been and what they've been up to.

Do I have a gambling problem?

You may have a gambling problem if you:

⇨ Feel the need to be secretive about your gambling. You might gamble in secret or lie about how much you gamble, feeling others won't understand or that you will surprise them with a big win.

⇨ Have trouble controlling your gambling. Once you start gambling, can you walk away? Or are you compelled to gamble until you've spent your last dollar, upping your bets in a bid to win lost money back?

⇨ Gamble even when you don't have the money. A red flag is when you are getting more and more desperate to recoup your losses. You may gamble until you've spent your last pound, and then move on to money you don't have – money to pay bills, credit cards or things for your children. You may feel pushed to borrow, sell or even steal things for gambling money. It's a vicious cycle. You may sincerely believe that gambling more money is the only way to win lost money back. But it only puts you further and further in the hole.

⇨ Family and friends are worried about you. Denial keeps problem gambling going. If friends and family are worried, listen to them carefully. Take a hard look at how gambling is affecting your life. It's not a sign of weakness to ask for help. Many older gamblers are reluctant to reach out to their adult children if they've gambled away their inheritance. But it's never too late to make changes for the better.

Treatment for problem gambling

Every gambler is unique and so needs a recovery programme tailored specifically to him or her. What works for one gambler won't necessarily work for you. The biggest step in treatment is realising you have a problem with gambling. It takes tremendous strength and courage to own up to this, especially if you have lost a lot of money and strained or broken relationships along the way. Don't despair, and don't try to go it alone. Many others have been in your shoes and have been able to break the habit.

Overcoming a gambling addiction or problem is never easy. But recovery is possible if you stick with treatment and seek support.

Group support for gambling addiction and problem gambling

Gamblers Anonymous is a 12 step recovery programme patterned after Alcoholics Anonymous. A key part of a 12-step programme is choosing a sponsor. A sponsor is a former gambler who has time and experience remaining free from addiction, and can often provide invaluable guidance and support.

Therapy for problem gambling

Cognitive-behavioural therapy for problem gambling focuses on changing unhealthy gambling behaviours and thoughts, such as rationalisations and false beliefs. It also teaches problem gamblers how to fight gambling urges, deal with uncomfortable emotions rather than escape through gambling, and solve financial, work and relationship problems caused by the addiction.

The goal of treatment is to 'rewire' the addicted brain by thinking about gambling in a new way. A variation of cognitive behavioural therapy, called the Four Steps Programme, has been used in treatment of compulsive gambling as well. The goal is to change your thoughts and beliefs about gambling in four steps; re-label, reattribute, refocus, and revalue.

Seeing a therapist does not mean you are weak or can't handle your problems. Therapy is for people who are smart enough to realise they need help. It can give you tools and support for reframing your thoughts that will last a lifetime.

Maintaining recovery for problem gambling and gambling addiction

As you may have noticed, quitting problem gambling is relatively easy. It's staying in recovery – making a permanent commitment to stay away from gambling – that is such a challenge. Maintaining recovery for problem gambling and gambling addiction is possible if you surround yourself with people to whom you're accountable, avoid tempting environments, give up control of your finances (at least at first) and find exciting or enjoyable activities to replace gambling.

Changing your lifestyle and making healthier choices

One way to stop yourself from problem gambling is to analyse what is needed for gambling to occur, work on removing these elements from your life and replace them with healthier choices. The four elements needed for problem gambling to continue are:

⇨ A decision: before gambling occurs, the decision to gamble has been made. If you have an urge to gamble: stop what you are doing and call someone, think about the consequences to your actions, tell yourself to stop thinking about gambling, and find something else to do immediately.

⇨ Money: gambling cannot occur without money. Get rid of your credit cards, let someone else be in charge of your money, have the bank make automatic payments for you, and keep a limited amount of cash on you at all times.

⇨ Time: gambling cannot occur if you don't have the time. Schedule enjoyable recreational time for yourself that has nothing to do with gambling, find time for relaxation, and plan outings with your family.

⇨ A game: without a game or activity to bet on there is no opportunity to gamble. Don't put yourself in tempting environments or locations. Tell the gambling establishments you frequent that you have a gambling problem and ask them to restrict you from betting at their casinos and establishments. Block online gambling sites on your computer.

Maintaining recovery from problem gambling or gambling addiction depends a lot on the reasons why you were gambling in the first place. Once you've quit gambling, reasons such as depression, loneliness or boredom will remain, so in order to maintain your recovery, you'll need to address these problems. There are alternative behaviours you can substitute for gambling. Some examples include those listed in the table below.

⇨ The above information is reprinted with kind permission from HelpGuide.org. Please visit www.helpguide.org for further information.

© Helpguide.org 2014

Reason for gambling	Sample substitute behaviours
To provide excitement, get a rush of adrenaline	Sport or a challenging hobby, such as mountain biking, rock climbing, or Go Kart racing
To be more social, overcome shyness or isolation	Counselling, enroll in a public speaking class, join a social group, connect with family and friends, volunteer, find new friends
To numb unpleasant feelings, not think about problems	Therapy, consult Helpguide's Bring Your Life into Balance toolkit
Boredom or loneliness	Find something you're passionate about such as art, music, sports or books then find others with the same interests
To relax after a stressful day	As little as 15 minutes of daily exercise can relieve stress. Or deep breathing, meditation, or massage
To solve money problems	The odds are always stacked against you so it's far better to seek help with debts from a credit counsellor

The social impact of problem gambling

By Elaine Smethurst

Anyone who gets caught up in the downward spiral of problem gambling finds only too soon that the negative impact on his or her life can be devastating. Finding money to gamble is usually the most immediate and obvious issue which brings with it enough problems, but in addition an all-consuming compulsion to gamble at any cost leads to difficulties which affect employment, quality of life, family relationships and mental and physical health.

And of course, problem gambling doesn't just affect the individual. It's estimated that for every problem gambler at least ten other family members, friends and colleagues are also directly affected. The negative impact on wider society is only just beginning to be recognised and an analysis of those problem gamblers in the Gordon Moody Association residential treatment programme during 2012 and 2013 gives the following insights:

Financial cost

The amounts gambled away varied between £5,000 and £3 million. Of those gambling in the range £10,000–£50,000, 59 people claimed to have gambled away a total amount of £1,225,194 with an average amount of £20,766 gambled per person.

Even for those with a job this is a sizeable amount to have to find on top of living expenses and, since the majority were unemployed (65% in 2013, 78% in 2012), all this gambling money had to be funded from other sources – borrowing from family and friends, high street money lenders, pawnshops and loan sharks.

Many Gordon Moody Association residents also report that families remortgage their houses and go into debt themselves in order to try and help sort out the problems of their loved one.

Many problem gamblers get into huge debt and often resort to illegal activities to fund their addiction including stealing from their loved ones and their employers as well as turning to other illegal ways of making money to gamble.

Those who are unable to cope with their debts may choose or be forced into bankruptcy and society then carries the rest of the debt. If court costs are involved this adds to the total financial cost.

Those who are unemployed and unable to work due to their addiction are surviving on state benefits which at the very minimum amount to £57.35 per week (Jobseekers Allowance) and may amount to a great deal more. Assuming six months unemployment and at the basic rate of benefit this is an additional cost of £1,491 per person for 18–24s and £1,882 for adults who are 25+.

Criminality

If a problem gambler turns to crime then police time, court costs, probation services and prison services and other support services need to be factored into the cost to society. The average annual overall cost of a prison place in England and Wales for the financial year 2011–12 was £37,649 (NOMS).

Health services

Whilst problem gambling has not until recently been identified officially as a health issue and little or no funding is currently available for treatment from the NHS, health services are often involved, as many problem gamblers develop physical and mental health issues as a result of stress and anxiety and the effects of other risk-taking behaviours.

The effects on children

Sadly, many family relationships breakdown as a result of problem gambling and children are the innocent victims not only because of the emotional distress created within the home but also often the loss of contact with their parent who leaves and the poverty which can result because of the behaviour of the problem gambler.

With this in mind it is clear to see that the issues and costs associated with any problem gambler can extend far beyond the basic financial cost and helping the recovery of one individual will have a much wider positive social impact.

16 April 2014

⇨ The above information is reprinted with kind permission from the Gordon Moody Association. Please visit www.gordonmoody.org.uk for further information.

Kids exposed to TV gambling adverts 211 times a year – as number soars by 1,444%

By Asa Bennett

Kids as young as four are being exposed to gambling adverts on TV more than 200 times a year, as official figures show that the amount of gambling ads has soared by 1,444% over the last eight years.

According to a shocking report by broadcasting regulator Ofcom, there has been a 15-fold increase in the number of gambling adverts on television over the last eight years, from 90,000 in 2005 to 1.39 million in 2012. The amount of television advertising represented by gambling has more than doubled from 1.7% to 4% over the period.

The report revealed how young children from the ages of 4 to 15 were exposed to TV gambling adverts 473 times in 2012, or 1.8 billion 'commercial impacts'.

The findings show the spread of gambling adverts on TV after the last Labour government decided in 2007 to allow such adverts to be broadcast before the 9pm watershed. Before this time, only football pools, bingo halls and the National Lottery could advertise.

Ofcom said the watchdog had carried out this research 'to help inform it about how television gambling advertising has changed since the market was liberalised by Parliament in 2007. This supports Ofcom's role in monitoring and understanding the markets it regulates.'

A spokesman for GamCare, a gambling charity offering support to vulnerable gamblers, said the 'massive increase' of TV gambling ads over the years has been 'pretty obvious'.

The spokesman added: 'Our concerns are that there's been a massive increase in wider exposure

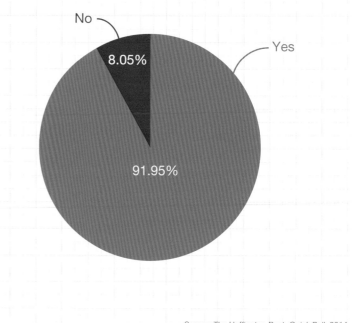

Are you worried about the spread of gambling ads?

No — 8.05%
Yes
91.95%

Source: The Huffington Post, *Quick Poll, 2014*

to gambling as a leisure activity. We of course don't judge that reality, but we do have concerns that it's exposing people who may not have otherwise sought out gambling as a leisure activity.'

Lib Dem MP Tessa Munt said the law needed to change to stop the 'insidious' rise of gambling adverts, adding: 'The real problem with these adverts is they make gambling seem normal.'

20 November 2013

⇨ The above information is reprinted with kind permission from The Huffington Post UK. Please visit www.huffingtonpost.co.uk for further information.

Scientists identify part of brain linked to gambling addiction

New research reveals that brain damage affecting the insula – an area with a key role in emotions – disrupts errors of thinking linked to gambling addiction.

The research, led by Dr Luke Clark from the University of Cambridge, was published on 7 April 2014 in the journal *PNAS*.

During gambling games, people often misperceive their chances of winning due to a number of errors of thinking called cognitive distortions. For example, 'near-misses' seem to encourage further play, even though they are no different from any other loss. In a random sequence like tossing a coin, a run of one event (heads) makes people think the other outcome (tails) is due next; this is known as the 'gambler's fallacy'.

There is increasing evidence that problem gamblers are particularly prone to these erroneous beliefs. In this study, the researchers examined the neurological basis of these beliefs in patients with injuries to different parts of the brain.

'While neuroimaging studies can tell us a great deal about the brain's response to complex events, it's only by studying patients with brain injury that we can see if a brain region is actually needed to perform a given task,' said Dr Clark.

For the study, the researchers gave patients with injuries to specific parts of the brain (the ventromedial prefrontal cortex, the amygdala or the insula) two different gambling tasks: a slot machine game that delivered wins and 'near-misses' (like a cherry one position from the jackpot line), and a roulette game involving red or black predictions, to elicit the gambler's fallacy. For the control groups, they also had patients with injuries to other parts of the brain as well as healthy participants undergo the gambling tasks.

All of the groups with the exception of the patients with insula damage reported a heightened motivation to play following near-misses in the slot machine game, and also fell prey to the gambler's fallacy in the roulette game.

Clark added: 'Based on these results, we believe that the insula could be hyperactive in problem gamblers, making them more susceptible to these errors of thinking. Future treatments for gambling addiction could seek to reduce this hyperactivity, either by drugs or by psychological techniques like mindfulness therapies.'

Gambling is a widespread activity: 73% of people in the UK report some gambling involvement in the past year* and around 50% play games other than the National Lottery. For a small proportion of players (around 1–5%), their gambling becomes excessive, resulting in features seen in addiction. Problem gambling is associated with both debt and family difficulties as well as other mental health problems like depression.

*2010 British Gambling Prevalence Survey

8 April 2014

⇨ The above information is reprinted with kind permission from the University of Cambridge. Please visit www.cam.ac.uk for further information.

Incorrect claims gambling is caused by brain damage

'The gambler's fallacy explained? Misguided belief in the big win just around the corner could be down to brain damage', The Independent *incorrectly reported.*

The news is based on a small experimental study that assessed performance in two gambling games in healthy people, and in people with damage to specific regions of the brain.

One of the games was a slot machine game, which assessed motivation to continue playing after a near miss. The other was a roulette game. This game assessed gambler's fallacy, the belief that past results have an influence on future results. The researchers looked to see whether participants chose a colour (red/blue) after runs of that colour outcome.

In healthy people, compared with 'full misses', near misses increased motivation to continue playing the slot machine game. In the roulette wheel game, healthy people were less likely to choose a colour after a run of the same colour.

However, people with brain damage to the insula (a region of the brain believed to be involved in feelings and emotional responses) had reduced motivation to play the slot machine task following near misses compared with full misses, and did not display classic gambler's fallacy effect on a roulette wheel game.

Further larger studies are required, but overall the results of this study suggest that the insula region of the brain may play a role in the responses to gambling, as well as playing a role in how we make decisions in different settings.

Where did the story come from?

The study was carried out by researchers from the University of Cambridge and University College London in the UK and the University of Iowa and University of Southern California in the US. It was funded by the UK Medical Research Council and the US National Institute of Neurological Disorders and Stroke, and the National Institute on Drug Abuse.

The study was published in the peer-reviewed journal, *Proceedings of the National Academy of Sciences (PNAS)*.

The news was generally well covered by the media, although it is yet to be determined whether the insula is overactive in people with gambling addiction, as suggested by the Mail Online. *The Independent*'s initial online headline – that the gambler's fallacy could be down to 'brain damage' – was later updated to more correctly say that the issue could be related to 'brain activity'. The print version of the paper ran the more subtle if still slightly awry headline 'Feeling lucky? Now scientists can tell gamblers why'.

What kind of research was this?

This was an experimental study that aimed to compare performance in two gambling games in healthy people and in people with injuries in specific regions of the brain. The aim was to see which brain regions could be involved in two gambling distortions: the response to 'near-miss' outcomes and the processing of random sequences.

A study such as this is hypothesis generating – that is, it suggests theories as to what parts of the brain may be involved in responses to gambling. However, it does not provide proof that these areas are responsible for problem gambling and further research is needed.

What did the research involve?

The researchers compared people with brain injuries in specific target regions:

⇨ 17 with damage to the ventromedial prefrontal cortex [vmPFC]

⇨ eight with damage to the insula

⇨ six with damage to the amygdala.

They compared these with 16 healthy people and 13 people with brain injuries that did not affect those specific regions.

Participants were given a computer slot machine and roulette games.

The slot machine game was programmed to deliver near-misses, as well as wins and full-misses. Half the time participants were asked to select a play icon from one of six alternatives, the rest of the time the computer selected a play icon. After the play icon was selected, participants were asked to rate their chances of winning. The participants then received a win or no-win result. After each play, participants were asked how pleased they were with the result and how much they wanted to continue playing the game.

Participants played 90 times on the roulette wheel game. The roulette wheel displayed an equal number of red and blue segments, and before each game the participant had to choose a colour. This game assessed gambler's fallacy. The gambler's fallacy is a bias in the processing of randomness, whereby recent consecutive outcomes are considered less likely to repeat, and conversely, outcomes that have not occurred in the recent history are perceived as 'due'. The researchers looked to see whether participants chose a colour (red/blue) after runs of that colour outcome.

What were the basic results?

Slot machine game

When participants selected the play icon for themselves, rather than the computer selecting it for them, they rated their chances of winning as higher. The researchers suggest that this is consistent with the illusion of control that leads from personal choice. There was no difference between people with injuries in specific target regions, healthy people and people with other brain injuries.

Participants were happiest with the result when they received a win, although response to a win was significantly reduced in people with injuries in specific target regions compared to people with other brain injuries. How pleased participants were with winning was not affected by whether they or the computer had selected the play icon.

Receiving a win increased motivation to continue. There was no difference between people with injuries in specific target regions, healthy people and people with other brain injuries, and motivation was not significantly affected by whether they or the computer had selected the play icon.

Compared with full misses, near misses also increased motivation to continue playing. However, people with brain injuries in specific target regions had reduced motivation to continue playing following near misses versus 'full misses' compared to healthy participants and participants with other brain injuries.

When the people with injuries in specific target regions were divided up, it was found that people with injuries in the insula had reduced motivation to play following a near miss than following a full miss. People with injuries in the vmPFC also had reduced motivation to play following a near miss than following a full miss, but the difference was smaller.

Roulette wheel game

In the roulette wheel game, participants chose each colour less after longer runs of the colour. This effect did not vary between groups.

However, when the people with injuries in specific target regions were divided up, it was found that people with injuries in the insula were more likely to choose a colour after longer runs of the same colour. This was different to people with injuries to the vmPFC and amygdala.

How did the researchers interpret the results?

The researchers conclude that, 'our findings indicate that the distorted cognitive processing of near-miss outcomes and event sequences may be ordinarily supported by the recruitment of the insula. Interventions to reduce insula reactivity could show promise in the treatment of disordered gambling.'

Conclusion

This experimental study in a small number of people with different brain injuries and a comparison group of healthy people, has found that people with brain damage to the insula (a region of the brain believed to be involved in feelings and emotional responses) had reduced motivation to play the slot machine task following near misses compared with full misses. These people also did not display classic gambler's fallacy effect on a roulette wheel game – in that they were not more likely to choose a blue after long runs of red or vice versa.

A study such as this suggests regions of the brain that may be involved in responses to gambling. However, it does not provide proof that any particular part of the brain causes gambling addiction. The study has involved only a small number of people, and comparing game performance in people with and without brain injuries does not reflect the real life scenario of gambling by people with gambling addiction.

This study could be followed up by carrying out brain imaging on people with known gambling problems to see which parts of their brain were active.

Overall, the results of this small study suggest that the insula region of the brain may play a role in responses to gambling, as well as playing a role in how we make decisions in different settings, but much further research is required.

Analysis by Bazian. Edited by NHS Choices.

8 April 2014

⇨ The above information is reprinted with kind permission from NHS Choices. Please visit www.nhs.uk for further information.

Chapter

3

Gambling and you

Legal ages

As a general rule, the minimum legal age for gambling in the UK is 18 years old. This applies to adult gaming centres, betting shops, bingo halls, casinos, racetracks and online gambling. The exceptions to this are the National Lottery and scratchcards – you're allowed to take part in these from the age of 16.

However, some gaming machines, such as coin pushers, teddy grabbers and some lower stakes fruit machines in family entertainment centres and amusement arcades don't have a minimum legal age at all. These might not seem risky because usually you'll only lose between 2p and £1 in a single game, but very few of us ever stop at one. It's incredibly easy to keep popping pound coins into change machines, then dropping the change into these games. Before you know it you've spent twenty pounds on a keyring or cheap toy car. Is it really worth it?

Any venue that provides gambling activities with a minimum legal age must stick to rules designed to prevent underage gambling.

What do young people gamble on?

Young people take part in all forms of gambling. The most common types for young people between 11 and 16 are the lottery, scratchcards and slot machines, and making bets or playing cards with friends, with either cash or other items at stake.

⇨ The above information is reprinted with kind permission from GamCare. GamCare is the leading provider of information, advice, support and free counselling for the prevention and treatment of problem gambling. GamCare staff are fully trained and give confidential guidance to anyone affected by a gambling problem. Freephone 0808 8020133 or visit www.gamcare.org.uk for further information.

© GamCare 2014

Underage gambling: a summary of key findings

- 15% of 11- to 15-year-olds gambled in the past week, a fall from 18% in 2012.

- 5% of 11- to 15-year-olds bought a National Lottery ticket or scratchcard in the past week, a fall from 7% in 2012.

- Of those playing National Lottery games, 9% said they personally handed the money over at the till. This equates to 1% of 11- to 15-year-olds personally purchasing tickets.

- 76% who've bought tickets in a shop said their parents handed over the money at the till.

- 80% who've visited the National Lottery website did so to check their parents' numbers.

- 50% of children said they bought tickets at the weekend last time they played, and 24% during school holidays.

- 60% of past-week Lotto players had spent £2 or less.

- Rates of play on 'real' gambling games are higher among those who have played practice games for free, suggesting that games have a similar appeal. Those who gamble on one type of game are more likely to gamble on other games.

Source: Young People Omnibus 2013, *A research study on gambling amongst 11–16-year-olds on behalf of the National Lottery Commission. Ipsos Mori, 2013*

Gambling regulation

The UK gambling industry offers diverse forms of gambling to the public including casino games, sports-betting, bingo and gaming machines. All these are available on the high street and online from operators who hold the necessary licences issued by the Gambling Commission and local authorities, although in the case of online supplies the operator may be licensed in an offshore jurisdiction. You are advised to check on an operator's website which of its products is licensed where, and whether you are satisfied from a review of the regulator's site that you will be adequately protected if you play. Unfortunately not all online licensing regimes have the same standards, albeit there are a number that have very similar systems to the UK.

The UK gambling industry employs some 214,000 people. In addition to the standard taxes that non-gambling businesses pay, the gambling industry pays betting and gaming duties. In 2009 these duties amounted to £1.4 billion. The industry is proud of its contribution to the British economy. But the industry is also mindful of its social responsibilities.

Licensed gambling operators comply with stringent licensing conditions designed to protect and help problem gamblers. For example, there are maximum limits on stakes and prizes, and procedures are available to enable customers to have themselves excluded from premises where gambling is available.

For a small number of people gambling may become a problem. The seriousness of the industry's commitment to protecting and helping problem gamblers is reflected in the size of the voluntary contribution that it makes to fund gambling related research, education and treatment. In 2012–2013 the industry contributed over £5 million via the Responsible Gambling Trust, and is expected to contribute over £6 million in 2013–2014. The gambling industry is unique in funding relevant research, education and treatment activities on this voluntary basis. GambleAware™ itself is owned and operated by the Responsible Gambling Trust. More information about the Responsible Gambling Trust and its work can be found at www. responsiblegamblingtrust.org.uk. For information about the Gambling Commission, regulators of the British gambling industry, please go to www. gamblingcommission.gov.uk.

Legal ages

As a general rule, the minimum legal age for gambling in the UK is 18 years old. This applies to adult gaming centres, betting shops, bingo halls, casinos, racetracks and online gambling. The exceptions to this are the National Lottery, lotteries and football pools – you're allowed to take part in these from the age of 16 as well as some non-commercial gambling, or low stakes and prizes gambling. However, some gaming machines, such as coin pushers, teddy grabbers and some lower stakes fruit machines in family entertainment centres and amusement arcades don't have a minimum legal age and are open to anyone. Note that a person who is over the age of 16 and under 18 who participates in gambling (not permitted under these exemptions) is also guilty of a criminal offence. Again, participation in any gambling product offered offshore may be subject to different rules, and it is advisable to check the position.

Social gaming

Currently in the UK, games that do not enable you to win anything in money or money's worth fall outside regulation and the parameters of our remit. However, the worldwide popularity of some of these games which are constructed be highly interactive, sociable and compelling (particularly where they bear a resemblance to play for real casino games), may ultimately prompt regulators in the UK and elsewhere to regulate.

⇨ The above information is reprinted with kind permission from the Responsible Gambling Trust. Please visit www.gambleaware. co.uk for further information.

A gambling policy manifesto for 2014–15

Gambling Watch UK Manifesto 2014–15.

By Jim Orford, Emeritus Professor of Clinical & Community Psychology, University of Birmingham

This is a first draft so all comments are welcome. The aim is to use it later on to question the political parties about their gambling policies in the run up to the 2015 general election. What do you think should be in the shopping list of proposals?

1. In government, gambling should be seen as a cross-department issue, with the Department of Health, Home Office, and Department for Culture Media and Sport having regular and ongoing inputs. The minister with chief responsibility for gambling should be a Department of Health minister, reflecting an important shift towards seeing gambling first and foremost as a public health matter.

2. Fixed Odds Betting Terminals (FOBTs), which offer high-stake gambling on virtual casino-type games, should not be permitted in venues outside casinos. This would deal with what has become the most dangerous form of highly accessible gambling and would reverse the process whereby high street betting shops are becoming town centre 'mini-casinos'.

3. Any proposed new form of gambling, mode or type of venue, should be subject to a full social, health and economic impact assessment. This would be designed to avoid the kind of mistake that was made when, some years ago, FOBTs were permitted in British betting shops.

4. A minimum age of 18 years should apply to all electronic gambling machines (excluding coin-push and prize-grab games) whatever their stake and prize sizes. This would remove the anomaly whereby children and young people in Britain, unlike in other jurisdictions, are permitted to play on category D machines. The present position is inconsistent with a major purpose of the Gambling Act 2005, to protect children from harm from gambling.

5. Television advertising of any form of gambling should not be permitted before 9 p.m. This would also bring regulations more into line with the principle of protecting children from harm.

6. A national programme of treatment for problem gambling should be put in place ensuring that health services in all areas include facilities for the treatment of those with gambling problems and for their families.

7. The regular, three-yearly, British Gambling Prevalence Survey should be reintroduced, but with a better balance between questions about gamblers and questions about the products they gamble on.

8. The present system of financing gambling treatment, prevention and research through an annual voluntary levy of approximately £5–£6 million administered by the industry-led Responsible Gambling Trust, does not command respect and should be reformed. It should be replaced by a mandatory levy, including a proportionate contribution from National Lottery takings, substantially increased in size (to at least £25 million annually), and administered by a body that is completely independent of the industry.

8 April 2014

⇨ The above information is reprinted with kind permission from Gambling Watch UK. Please visit www.gamblingwatchuk.org for further information or contact j.f.orford@bham.ac.uk.

© Gambling Watch UK 2014

Playing with fire: peril of Britain's obsession with gambling

By Jim Orford, Emeritus Professor of Clinical & Community Psychology, University of Birmingham.

The Government has this week announced increased powers for local authorities to refuse new licences for betting shops and impose extra controls on machine gambling. The background to this is concern about the so-called Fixed Odds Betting Terminals (FOBTs) in betting shops. Unlike slot or fruit machines, where the maximum stake per play is £2, FOBTs allow the playing of casino-type games such as roulette, and the maximum stake is £100. They have rapidly become the single most profitable form of British gambling. All types of gambling carry the potential for addiction to some degree but not all forms of gambling are equally addictive. Gambling machines are thought to be among the more addictive because of the speed of play, the 'random reinforcement' pay-out schedule which is particularly habit forming, the prospect of a jackpot win encouraged by frequent smaller wins (really 'losses disguised as wins') and frequent 'near wins', plus machine design features which enhance the sights and sounds associated with winning or which encourage the 'illusion of control'. The dangerousness of gambling machines has been mitigated in Britain by keeping stakes low. But FOBTs slipped in through a loophole in the law about ten years ago and there is now considerable evidence of the harm they are causing to gamblers and their families and communities, particularly in more deprived areas.

The Government is under increasing pressure to do something about them and the betting shop industry is on the defensive. The response of the Association of British Bookmakers has been to produce a Code of Conduct, which allows players to set spending and time limits and gives an alert and a 30-second time-out if a limit is reached. This is weak and unlikely to have much impact. Most importantly, it leaves in place, unaltered in all essential respects, these fast, high-stake, highly addictive machines.

The necessary action would be far stronger. Among the options are: the maximum stake allowed per play should be reduced from the current £100 to £2, which is the standard maximum for other kinds of gambling machine; the removal of FOBTs from high-street betting shops altogether, confining them to casinos; giving local authorities the powers – which they currently lack – to control gambling on their high streets, including the power to vote to make an area an 'FOBT-free zone'; and/or 'mandatory pre-commitment', whereby a player would be required (not just invited) to set a personal spending limit at the outset of play, and would be excluded from playing for a longer period if that limit was reached.

Opportunities for gambling in Britain have increased very considerably in the last 20 years and were given further encouragement with the passing of the liberalising 2005 Gambling Act and the passing of the Government lead on gambling from the Home Office to the Department for Culture, Media and Sport, with the Department of Health playing a negligible role. The latest *British Gambling Prevalence Survey*, carried out in 2009–10, found that between one-third and half a million British adults experienced a gambling problem in the previous 12 months, which represents a sizeable public health problem similar in magnitude to the problem of the misuse of Class A drugs. It also found that, although most of the population is not in favour of prohibiting gambling, attitudes are generally quite negative towards gambling in all sections of the population.

What particularly motivated me to set up the Gambling Watch UK website is the need for a public space for critical reflection and comment on the growth of gambling in Britain. Criticism of the vigorous promotion of gambling by those who have a financial interest in promoting it, and of the Government which is failing to show necessary caution in its support for the gambling industry, can be mounted on the grounds that gambling produces harmful consequences (the consequentialist argument) and on the grounds that gambling, particularly in certain forms, and its prominent advertising – for example, on television before 9.00 p.m. – is not in keeping with values most people wish to support (the values-based argument). It is difficult to find the space to present such views and to have them listened to respectfully as part of the national debate we should be having. This is partly because there is no organisation speaking on the subject of gambling which is independent of government or the gambling – providing industry. Particularly concerning from a university perspective, the main source of research funds is voluntary donations by the gambling industry and no way has yet been found to make the disbursement of those funds properly independent of the industry. Meanwhile we have a situation in which individuals and organisations with special knowledge and expertise, who might speak out against the harmful expansion of gambling, have in effect been silenced because of their links with the industry. We also badly need a national programme of treatment for problem gambling ensuring that there are services in all areas for the treatment of those with gambling problems and for their families.

1 May 2014

⇨ The above information is reprinted with kind permission from Gambling Watch UK. Please visit www.gamblingwatchuk.org for further information or contact j.f.orford@bham.ac.uk.

Gambling protections and controls

Player protection measures

Gambling operators are already required to maintain certain standards of social responsibility. The Gambling Commission's Licence Conditions and Codes of Practice set out a number of social responsibility conditions which operators must comply with or face licence suspension, revocation or the imposition of a financial penalty.

However, it is clear that some people have encountered considerable problems with their gambling despite the obligations on operators to supervise their customers. A combination of high stakes and natural game volatility (where the player might be encouraged by the odd small win to put at risk high stakes) can generate significant losses in a short space of time. We want players who use gaming machines to be in control of the choices they make. This is particularly important for users of category B2 gaming machines, where it is possible for individuals to place higher stakes.

For these reasons, the Government is adopting a precautionary approach to high stakes gaming machines on the high street. Our measures are justified on a proportionate, targeted basis to help people remain in control of their gambling. At the heart of our approach are measures designed to give players better information, and to provide break points and pauses for thought to help people stay in control.

The Government intends to:

⇨ Require those accessing higher stakes (over £50) to use account-based play or load cash over the counter. Requiring better interaction between customer and operator for those engaged in high stake play improves opportunities for more effective provision of information and interventions.

To support this measure Government wants:

⇨ All larger betting shop operators to offer account-based play. This will allow account holders to track

and monitor their own play via statements, and enable targeted interventions in accordance with operators' licence conditions.

There are significant advantages to this approach. Account-based play allows players access to up-to-date and accurate information which can reduce biased or irrational gambling-related decisions and help people maintain control. The Government considers account summaries or activity statements may be a particularly effective way of giving clear and accurate information regarding game play and patterns of net expenditure. We expect larger gambling operators to encourage take up among their customers.

Making payments over the counter rather than on the machine directly can provide opportunities for intervention which may give players a reality check. This approach emphasises consumer control which is particularly important given that some experts believe that a lack of control may be a determinant of problem gambling.

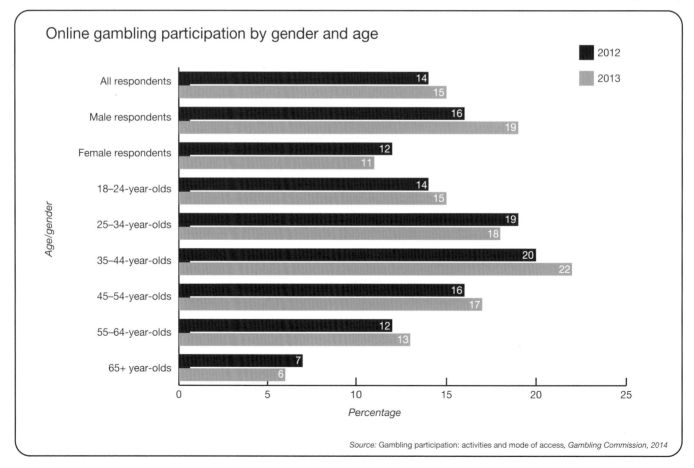

Online gambling participation by gender and age

Age/gender	2012	2013
All respondents	14	15
Male respondents	16	19
Female respondents	12	11
18–24-year-olds	14	15
25–34-year-olds	19	18
35–44-year-olds	20	22
45–54-year-olds	16	17
55–64-year-olds	12	13
65+ year-olds	7	6

Percentage

Source: Gambling participation: activities and mode of access, *Gambling Commission, 2014*

The Government also considers that pre-commitment (where players are required to make a decision about how much, or how long, they are willing to spend before beginning play) can be effective in helping customers to make clear and well-informed decisions about their gambling before they begin play, rather than when frustrated, disappointed, excited or chasing their losses.

The betting industry introduced new player protection measures on gaming machines from 1 March 2014. These measures include suspensions in play if voluntary limits are reached and alerts that tell players when they've been playing for 30 minutes or when £250 has been spent. While a step in the right direction, the Government believes measures which protect players and enhance supervision should be toughened and made mandatory.

The Gambling Commission is undertaking a review of its licence conditions and codes of practice with a view to:

⇨ Requiring all players of fixed odds betting terminals to be presented with a choice to set limits before play.

⇨ Ensuring regular warning messages and pauses in play on gaming machines in betting shops to prompt players to actively consider their behaviour, and help them to remain in control.

⇨ Working with industry to oversee the introduction of an advanced system of voluntary self-exclusion. This will allow customers to make a single request to exclude themselves from betting shops on a wider basis than is currently possible.

The Government fully supports the Gambling Commission in its review of licence conditions and codes of practice. It is anticipated that changes brought forward as a result of the Gambling Commission's review of licence conditions and codes of practice will be implemented from autumn 2014. The Government will prepare the necessary impact assessment and regulatory measures to implement these changes. We expect changes to take effect from October 2014.

Gambling advertising

The codes which govern gambling advertising are now applied across a much changed gambling landscape with the availability and promotion of new products which were not anticipated when the codes were devised. It is timely that the codes are re-examined to ensure that existing controls keep pace with developments in the market, provide adequate protection – especially to children and the vulnerable – and remain consistent with public expectations about gambling advertising.

There is some evidence that gambling advertising may maintain or exacerbate already existing gambling problems. The Government wants the industry and its regulators to carefully reconsider whether the tone, content and volume of gambling adverts is appropriate for general audiences and meets societal expectations, especially where adverts offer financial inducements or encourage 'in play' and other instantly accessible online gambling.

The Government has initiated the following work:

⇨ The Remote Gambling Association will make recommendations to government on any changes needed to the industry voluntary code, including on the suitability of the 9 p.m watershed arrangements.

⇨ The Committee of Advertising Practice and the Broadcast Committee of Advertising Practice will evaluate the latest evidence in relation to gambling advertising and problem gambling to consider what regulatory implications arise as a result.

⇨ The Advertising Standards Authority will report on the proportionality, robustness and consistency of its enforcement action on the gambling rules.

⇨ The Gambling Commission will ensure that its current review of licence conditions and codes of practice (which includes a focus on free bets and bonuses) ensures that all gambling advertising continues to comply with the licensing objectives of the Gambling Act 2005.

This work will be complete by the end of 2014. The Government retains powers under the Gambling Act 2005 to make regulations about gambling advertising.

Education

The young are confronted with more opportunities to gamble than ever before. These opportunities arise through online gambling and are increasingly marketed online and via social media, as well as bricks and mortar outlets found on the high street. In addition, young people are offered social gambling on social network Internet sites and mobile devices, which offer activities similar to gambling where significant amounts of time or money can be spent (although money or money's worth cannot be won).

We know that problem gambling – whilst relatively low in the UK – is highest amongst the 16–24 age group and therefore we must do more to help younger people prepare and educate themselves around how to engage with such activities in a socially responsible way. And we look to the industry to do more to protect those under age from exposure to gambling promotions.

The Government will:

⇨ Establish a £2 million programme funded by industry to promote responsible gambling, launching in the summer of 2014.

⇨ Work with the industry to explore how a Think 25 initiative could help prevent underage access to gambling products across the gambling landscape.

⇨ The above information is reprinted with kind permission from the Department for Culture Media & Sport. Please visit www.gov.uk for further information.

Budget 2014: bookmakers hit by triple tax whammy

William Hill and Ladbrokes shares dive on surprise 25% duty rate for fixed-odds betting machines, extension of the horse race betting levy and a 15% online gaming tax.

By Nathalie Thomas

Investors in Britain's biggest bookmakers ran for cover as they digested a new 25% higher tax rate for controversial fixed-odds gaming machines, which is expected to cost the betting industry an additional £335 million over the next five years.

Bookies such as William Hill, Ladbrokes and Gala Coral face a triple whammy of tax increases, as the Chancellor also announced plans to extend the horse race betting levy to gambling companies based offshore.

'Bookies such as William Hill, Ladbrokes and Gala Coral face a triple whammy of tax increases'

This could mean that bets placed through bookies' online operations, predominantly situated overseas, could also be subject to the levy, which currently only applies to bets placed on UK horse racing at high street betting shops.

A separate 15% online gaming tax, which will take effect from December 1, was also confirmed in the Budget.

Shares in William Hill plunged 7% to 351.5p, making it one of the biggest fallers in the FTSE 100, while Ladbrokes' shares dropped 12% to 140.4p.

Bookies were in a state of shock over the tax hit on fixed-odds betting terminals (FoBTs) in particular. The machines, which have been dubbed the 'crack cocaine of gambling' by campaigners, have been the subject of a recent political outcry, with the Labour Party calling for curbs.

The industry has been fearing a regulatory crackdown on FoBTs, also known as 'B2' machines, but the Government on Wednesday responded to the growing concern over the terminals by creating a new 25%higher tax rate.

Since February 1 2013, all gaming machines in betting shops have been subject to a 20% tax rate, which has already cost the industry £50 million.

The Association of British Bookmakers said: 'The licensed bookmaking industry is the only sector in the UK that pays more in tax than it generates in profits. The Government's desire to continue to soak the industry undermines our ability to continue to support horse and greyhound racing.'

One industry source accused the Chancellor of using the betting industry as a 'political football'.

FOBTs feature casino games, typically roulette, and in theory allow punters to stake £100 every 20 seconds.

Jeffrey Harwood, analyst at Oriel Securities, expects the higher rate will wipe 14% off Ladbrokes' pre-tax profits and 5% from William Hill's earnings.

Mr Harwood added that the policy, which will come into effect on March 1 2015, is likely to hit independent betting shops even harder and will potentially result in closures.

The announcement prompted William Hill to release a statement to the London Stock Exchange, saying that had the tax applied to its last financial year, it would have cost the company £16 million.

A spokesman for Ladbrokes said: 'A further £75 million tax hit on an industry that already contributes £1 billion and makes profits of just £600 million. The pips are squeeking – we now need a period of stability to let us continue to generate our employment and tax levels while delivering to shareholders.'

David Jennings, analyst at Davy, said that with three tax increases focussed on the sector, it is hard not to conclude that the Government 'has it in' for the bookies.

The Treasury expects to raise £335 million through the crackdown on FOBTs over the next five years, Budget documents show. The Department for Culture Media and Sport is also assessing how best to regulate B2 gaming machines, with a report due to be published before Easter.

Despite the bad news for bookies, the numbers came up for bingo halls as the Chancellor cut the rate of bingo duty in half to 10% from June 30.

Rank Group, the owner of 97 Mecca Bingo clubs in Britain, responded to the cut with plans for three further bingo clubs. Rank's shares jumped almost 7% to 154p on the news.

19 March 2014

⇨ The above information is reprinted with kind permission from *The Telegraph*. Please visit www.telegraph.co.uk for further information.

Gamblers to get warnings when they spend too much

Customers will get alerts when they are spending too much time or money on so-called 'crack cocaine' betting terminals under a new code of conduct.

Gamblers playing gaming machines in betting shops will get a warning after 30 minutes or when they have spent £250 under a new code of conduct that comes into force today. It follows warnings that players could blow £100 every 20 seconds on new high-speed, high-stakes machines.

The Association of British Bookmakers said the code would help tackle problem gambling. It also allows gamblers to set limits on how much time and money they spend. Staff will be alerted when the limit is reached and the gaming machine will force a 30-second break in play. The ABB claims this is a world first.

Chief executive Dirk Vennix said the initiative 'forms part of the industry's ongoing, proactive efforts to be socially responsible, to tackle problem gambling and to ensure a duty of care towards every customer'.

'Crack-cocaine' gaming machines

Earlier this month, the Responsible Gaming Trust, a charity funded by bookmakers, announced a review into the spread of the so-called 'crack cocaine' high-stakes betting terminals. The research will look into consumer behaviour and the risk of addiction, as well as examining whether gambling machines are more common in poorer areas.

David Cameron has called the issue a 'problem that needs looking at' but has ruled out allowing councils the right to ban the fixed-odds terminals. A recent study by the Gambling Commission showed that there were more than 33,000 in the UK making over £1.5 billion for bookies every year.

The ABB says the technology to enable the new measures is being put into in every machine across England and Wales but that testing and installation requirements mean they will take up to six months to introduce.

'Greater protection for players'

The measures have been welcomed by the gambling advice service GamCare. Its chief executive Dirk Hansen said that it would offer 'greater protections for players, encouraging responsible play', and added that it would raise 'awareness amongst betting shop customers about the help that is available for problem gambling.'

The Government Minister in charge of gambling, Helen Grant, called the new code a positive step but said more could be done. 'We want there to be a competitive gambling sector but not at the expense of public protection.'

28 February 2014

⇨ The above information is reprinted with kind permission from Channel 4 news. Please visit www. channel4.com for further information.

© Channel 4 2014

Key facts

⇨ When you flip a coin, the probability of it landing on heads is the same as the probability of it landing on tails, so you could say that it has a 50% chance or it's 50/50. (page 3)

⇨ The odds of winning the National Lottery jackpot are about one in 14 million. (page 3)

⇨ The EuroMillions is drawn every Tuesday and Friday and requires a player to pick five main numbers from one to 50 and two lucky star numbers from one to 11. You can win a lot more in this game, but the odds of winning the jackpot are one in over 116 million. (page 4)

⇨ Two per cent of young people in the UK (that's 60,000 young people) are likely to be struggling with a gambling problem this very moment. (page 5)

⇨ The Gambling Commission, using data provided by bookmakers, estimated there were 33,284 FOBTs in betting shops located across the UK in 2012. The declared gross profit from these machines was £1.42 billion last year, meaning the average weekly profit per machine was £825, up from £760 in 2011. (page 6)

⇨ In 2012–13, the Government received £1.7 billion in betting and gaming duties. (page 6)

⇨ The latest results [from the Gambling Commission) show that 55% of the UK gambles, down from 57% in 2012. (page 6)

⇨ In 2012/13 GamCare answered 16,168 calls from problem gamblers and people affected by gambling, an increase of 2.8% from the previous year. (page 10)

⇨ The number of people gambling online increased from 23% in 2011/12 to 26% in 2012/13. (page 10)

⇨ A 2011 study of more than 2,700 British secondary students found that 15 per cent had played free gambling games during the week prior to the survey. (page 11)

⇨ Two per cent of people between the ages of 11 and 15 had trouble controlling their gambling behaviour. This was equivalent to 60,000 secondary students in Britain. (page 11)

⇨ 50 per cent of the profits made by high-street bookies now come from the 33,000 FOBTs across Britain. (page 12)

⇨ In 2001, the first FOBT was introduced to the UK, by 2005 there were 20,000, and by 2013 there were 33,000 FOBTs in the UK. (page 14)

⇨ In total, almost two-thirds (62%) of betting shops are in areas with lower than average levels of deprivation. (page 19)

⇨ The number of betting shops increased by just 1.3% in 2013. (page 19)

⇨ In 2012, more than £5 billion was gambled on high-speed, high-stakes gambling machines in northern England cities and London boroughs with high levels of unemployment. (page 20)

⇨ The profit made by betting shops, known as the gross gambling yield, in the 50 poorest constituencies was just over £173 million, according to Fairer Gambling, which gleaned the figures from analysis of industry data. (page 20)

⇨ Compared with the UK population as a whole, where problem gambling affects 0.7% of people, the level of problem gambling among homeless people was 11.6%. (page 22)

⇨ According to the Gordon Moody Association, the amount that people gamble varies between £5,000 and £3 million. Of those gambling in the range £10,000 – £50,000, 59 people claimed to have gambled away a total amount of £1,225,194 with an average amount of £20,766 gambled per person. (page 27)

⇨ According to the Young People Omnibus, 2013, 15% of 11- to 15-year-olds gambled in the week before taking the survey, a fall from 18% in 2012. (page 32)

⇨ The UK gambling industry employs some 214,000 people. (page 33)

Bookmaker

A bookmaker's job is to take bets, calculate odds and pay out money when someone wins a bet.

Casino

A casino is an entertainment venue where various forms of gambling are offered. Casinos may include tables for games such as poker and roulette, as well as fruit machines. Bets are placed with chips (small plastic discs used to represent money). Chips can be bought and exchanged for money on entering and leaving the casino.

Fixed Odds Betting Terminal (FOBT)

An electromechanical device that allows people to bet on the outcome of a game or event with fixed odds. FOBTs have been highly criticised for their potential to develop addiction among players and have even been called the 'crack cocaine' of gambling. In response to this, in 2014, the Association of British Bookmakers introduced the facility for players to set a limit on the time they wish to play and the money they wish to spend.

Fruit machine

Fruit or slot machines are often found in pubs and casinos. Players insert money and are required to match symbols (usually fruit) in order to win the jackpot.

Gambling

An activity in which one or more persons take part, where a 'stake' (most often money) is placed on the result of an event whose outcome is uncertain. Examples include betting on sporting events, lotteries, bingo or card games.

The Gambling Commission

The regulatory authority for gambling in the UK. The Gambling Commission was set up under the Gambling Act 2005, as an independent non-departmental public body to assist with compliance and enforcement of UK gambling licensing regulations. It is supported by the Department for Culture, Media & Sport.

Lottery

A lottery is a form of gambling based purely on chance. Numbers are drawn at random from a set range, and customers win if their pre-chosen numbers match the ones that are drawn. A fee is charged to enter the lottery and the jackpot is a percentage of the amount paid by entrants.

Online gambling

Placing bets or taking part in casino games over the Internet. Internet gambling can be more dangerous than traditional forms, as players are easily able to transfer large amounts of cash without leaving their home. Since the money is transferred electronically, it can seem less 'real' and debts build up more easily.

Problem gambling

When gambling becomes an addiction that starts to have a noticeable negative impact on someone's life, this is referred to as 'problem gambling'. It might affect relationships, employment or someone's financial situation; for example, they may acquire heavy debts, and the secretive nature of their addiction may put a strain on family relationships.

Remote gambling

Placing bets by remote means; for example, using a mobile phone or computer. The term 'remote' refers to the fact that players do not need to enter a bookmakers or casino to place their bet; they can gamble from any location.

The Remote Gambling Association (RGA)

Located in Brussels, the Remote Gambling Association (RGA) is a trade association whose members are all licensed for gambling purposes in Europe. Their key objectives are to promote a 'regulated and non-discriminatory environment in terrestrial gambling establishments' and to 'encourage high standards of probity and integrity within the betting and gaming industry'.

Spread betting

Spread betting is a high-risk form of gambling, where the odds are not fixed but fluctuate. Spread betting can be used on sporting events or the stock market, and involves wagering on a range (or spread) of outcomes rather than a fixed 'win or lose'. It reduces the control the gambler has over the amount that they lose, although for the same reason, winnings can be very large.

Assignments

Brainstorming

⇨ In small groups, discuss what you know about gambling. Consider the following questions:

- What is gambling?
- What forms does it take?
- What is problem gambling?
- What are Fixed Odds Betting Terminals (FOBT) and why do they pose a problem?

Research

⇨ Create a questionnaire that will examine the gambling habits of students in your year. You should aim to find out:

- How often people gamble
- What kind of gambling activities they pursue (scratchcards, horse racing, slot machines, etc.)
- How they gamble (online, in betting shops, etc.)
- Differences in gender.

Analyse your results and write a report that includes at least two graphs/visual representations of your data.

⇨ Research the amount of betting shops in your local area. In pairs, walk down your local high-street and count the number of shops in different categories (clothes, charity, eateries, etc.). Then calculate what percentage of the total number is made up of betting shops.

⇨ Research gambling laws in the UK and create a comprehensive guide that could be published on a website or printed as a leaflet and handed out to the public.

Design

⇨ Design an app that will help people who have gambling problems. Your app could be a self-help guide, or something more sophisticated (for example, something which would automatically cut-off a player's access to another app when they have spent a certain amount of money). Get creative!

⇨ Design a leaflet that will be distributed to parents of 11- to 16-year-olds to raise awareness of problem gambling among young people. You should include signs and symptoms of problem gambling and sources of help/advice.

⇨ Design a pop-up warning for a FOBT that will appear when the player has spent a significant amount of money. The warning should alert the player to the addictive nature of gambling and advise potential problem gamblers where they can go for help. The warning should be eye-catching and persuasive, ensuring gamblers are aware of the potential dangers of FOBTs.

Oral

⇨ *'Compared with the UK population as a whole, where problem gambling affects 0.7% of people, the level of problem gambling among homeless people [is] 11.6%.'*

In small groups, discuss why you think the level of problem gambling is higher among the homeless population. Make notes about your ideas and feedback to your class.

⇨ *'Remote gambling should be banned in order to protect the public from developing addictive behaviour.'*

Stage a class debate in which half of you argue in favour of the statement above and half of you argue against it.

⇨ *'Social media gaming is a gateway to Internet gambling'.*

Discuss in pairs and feedback to your class.

Reading/writing

⇨ Write a letter to your local MP suggesting that Fixed Odds Betting Terminals should be banned in the UK.

⇨ Write a blog post from the point of view of a young person who is struggling with controlling their desire to gamble.

⇨ Imagine you have a friend who has developed an addiction to scratchcards. What advice would you give him/her? Write your friend a supportive email.

⇨ Watch the film *Casino Royale*. Do you think this film glamourises gambling? Is it right to portray gambling as exciting and attractive to film audiences? Write a review of the film which includes your views on this moral dilemma.

⇨ Read the articles *Study highlights need for more social responsibility by online gaming industry* and *Study refutes claims that bookies prey on the poor* on pages 18 and 19. Do a little research and investigate who wrote each article. In no more than two pages of A4, explore the motives behind each piece. If it helps, you could discuss this in pairs before writing.

Acknowledgements

The publisher is grateful for permission to reproduce the material in this book. While every care has been taken to trace and acknowledge copyright, the publisher tenders its apology for any accidental infringement or where copyright has proved untraceable. The publisher would be pleased to come to a suitable arrangement in any such case with the rightful owner.

Images

All images courtesy of iStock, except page 4 © Nikkorz (Flickr) and page 28 © Michael Dorausch. Icon on page 41 © SimpleIcon.

Illustrations

Don Hatcher: pages 2 & 29. Simon Kneebone: pages 20 & 33. Angelo Madrid: pages 27 & 34.

Additional acknowledgements

Editorial on behalf of Independence Educational Publishers by Cara Acred.

With thanks to the Independence team: Mary Chapman, Sandra Dennis, Christina Hughes, Jackie Staines and Jan Sunderland.

Cara Acred

Cambridge

January 2015